DISABILITY, CULTURE, AND EQUITY SERIES

Alfredo J. Artiles, *Series Editor*

Dismantling Disproportionality in Practice

A Guide to Fostering Culturally Responsive Districts and Schools

María G. Hernández, Reed Swier, and
Hui-Ling Sunshine Malone

Foreword by Pedro A. Noguera

TEACHERS COLLEGE PRESS

TEACHERS COLLEGE | COLUMBIA UNIVERSITY
NEW YORK AND LONDON

Published by Teachers College Press,® 1234 Amsterdam Avenue, New York, NY 10027

Library of Congress Cataloging-in-Publication Data
Names: Hernández, María G., author. | Swier, Reed, author. | Malone, Hui-Ling S., author.
Title: Dismantling disproportionality in practice : a guide to fostering culturally responsive districts and schools / María G. Hernández, Reed Swier and Hui-Ling S. Malone ; foreword by Pedro A. Noguera.
Description: Second edition. | New York, NY : Teachers College Press, [2024] | Series: Disability, culture, and equity series | Includes bibliographical references and index. | Summary: "This resource offers processes and concrete tools to help school districts confront disproportionate outcomes of special education placement and exclusionary discipline for students of color"— Provided by publisher.
Identifiers: LCCN 2023056203 (print) | LCCN 2023056204 (ebook) | ISBN 9780807769447 (paperback) | ISBN 9780807769454 (hardcover) | ISBN 9780807782262 (ebook)
Subjects: LCSH: Educational equalization—United States. | Discrimination in education—United States. | Special education—United States. | Children with social disabilities—Education—United States. | Children of minorities— Education—United States. | Culturally relevant pedagogy—United States.
Classification: LCC LC213.2 .H47 2024 (print) | LCC LC213.2 (ebook) | DDC 379.2/6—dc23/eng/20240109
LC record available at https://lccn.loc.gov/2023056203
LC ebook record available at https://lccn.loc.gov/2023056204

ISBN 978-0-8077-6944-7 (paper)
ISBN 978-0-8077-6945-4 (hardcover)
ISBN 978-0-8077-8226-2 (ebook)

Printed on acid-free paper
Manufactured in the United States of America

We dedicate this book to students, families, communities, and educators who have made a commitment to fighting for racial equity and justice. You are our inspiration.

Contents

Contents

Foreword

The effort to advance equity in education is under attack throughout the country. Ironically, the threat comes from two unlikely sources: conservative activists who now equate equity with "woke politics" and perceive its pursuit as a threat to their political interests, and school and district leaders who are unable to devise strategies that lead to measurable advancements in equity.

This book has been written for the latter group: district leaders and educators who are trying to make a genuine effort to advance equity by reducing racial disparities in academic achievement (aka the so-called achievement gap) and eliminating the disproportionate placement of children of color in special education, in discipline referrals, and in remedial classes generally. This book will illuminate what it takes to begin generating measurable academic progress for all students.

Since the 2001 adoption of No Child Left Behind (NCLB), the pursuit of equity in education had been widely embraced by red and blue states alike, from a rhetorical standpoint at least. The law required school districts throughout the nation to reduce disparities in academic performance and to produce measurable evidence that all students, regardless of their backgrounds, were making academic progress. Of course, relying upon student test scores as the sole measure of progress is highly problematic; nonetheless, some districts embraced the equity challenge enthusiastically, and adopted plans, set goals, and implemented strategies. Many other districts were reluctant converts to equity work; they paid lip service to compliance with NCLB but did little to address the barriers to student learning. Both types of districts were required by law to comply with the mandates of NCLB, so at schools across the country mission statements affirming a commitment to serve all students were adopted. However, only in a few cases was genuine progress achieved.

Part of the reason for the lack of progress is that many educators did not have a clear understanding of what equity work entails. In many communities, lack of progress added to the sense that while equity is a laudable goal, it is largely unattainable. When district leaders failed to make progress in advancing equity, they often faced criticism and pressure from the parents of children who have historically been poorly treated and poorly served. Even when leaders claim that the strategies they have designed and championed will eventually help such students, their inability to produce solid evidence of improvement has made them vulnerable to criticism, and in some cases placed their jobs in jeopardy. In such communities, Black and Latinx parents, as well as parents whose children receive bilingual or special education, or whose children are simply poor, have grown increasingly frustrated with leaders who are perceived as caring but inept. When leaders talk equity but fail to deliver results, they are more likely to come under scrutiny and attack. Lack of a viable strategy for achieving progress has also contributed to paralysis, cynicism, and confusion among staff.

Slogans and lofty promises are not a substitute for viable efforts that produce results. While many education leaders have adopted strategic plans to assuage community concerns and made pronouncements that sound a lot like those of politicians who have called for "ending the soft bigotry of low expectations" or described education as the "civil rights issue of the 21st century," when rhetoric is not matched by results, the patience of those who have too often been poorly served begins to wear thin.

This book can be a source of relief for educators who are searching for guidance on how to advance equity work. It is a practical guide for those who want to serve children well and who seek to create classrooms and schools where children are challenged and supported. For those who seek greater clarity about how to advance equity in their schools, this book will be invaluable. Written by three experienced educators who have worked closely with schools in advancing equity for several years, the book provides clear guidance on how to address racial disparities in special education, school discipline practices, and achievement generally that have stymied many schools for years.

Given the political climate in the United States today, the timing of this book's release is of utmost importance. Equity cannot be defended by political statements alone. Action and evidence are needed to show doubters and critics that the goal of educating all students, regardless of their backgrounds, can be achieved. There is not a single school district in the United States that is allowed by law to abdicate its responsibility to serve all students enrolled in it. The fact that far too many fail to live up to this expectation, especially for those with the greatest needs, does not absolve them of the responsibility to find a way to do so.

In offering this book to the public, we are not naïve about the nature of the problem we are dealing with. We realize that America's schools more often than not reflect the inequities and injustice present in society. For this reason, challenging and eliminating racial disparities cannot be approached through technical solutions alone. Educators who seek to produce real progress must generate the will among their staff, identify the barriers that impede progress and eliminate them, and find the resources needed to serve all kinds of students. Too often, the reason why Black children continue to be placed in special education or disciplined at a disproportionate rate and the reason for the persistence of stagnant academic outcomes and lack of educational progress can be explained by what we might term the "normalization of failure." When racial biases are rooted in the assumption that some kids are simply incapable of learning and these beliefs are unchallenged, complacency and a lack of will to address the challenges facing historically marginalized students invariably sets in.

This book may not be helpful to educators who simply don't care or who are comfortable with the status quo and the predictable ways in which race and class determine patterns of student achievement. However, we know from our work with schools that there are many educators who do care and who are deeply disturbed by the lack of progress in their schools. For such educators, this book will be a tremendous resource and a guide that can be used to clarify what equity work entails. Armed with this knowledge and a resolve to stick with the work, compassionate educators can approach the challenges facing their students and their schools with clarity and a renewed sense of urgency.

—Pedro A. Noguera, PhD

Dean, Rossier School of Education, USC

Preface

The first two authors are trainers and technical assistance providers in state education agencies (SEAs) and local education agencies (LEAs) throughout the country. The third author is a former teacher and assistant professor of education at the University of California, Santa Barbara who specializes in culturally sustaining pedagogies and youth participatory research. Throughout the years the first two authors have left our families to meet and partner alongside amazing educators, parents, young people, and community members, whom we continue to be inspired by and who are an ongoing reminder of why we show up.

Dismantling race-based disproportionality is a moral responsibility that *everyone* has. We have made a lifetime commitment to a moral imperative that the only way we can get to an equitable just schooling system and society is by dismantling the harm and exclusion that has occurred and continues to happen in schooling for students of color (in particular Black, Indigenous/Native, and Latinx), students with an Individualized Education Program (IEP), multilingual learners, and students holding these intersecting identities.

The impetus for *Dismantling Disproportionality in Practice: A Guide to Fostering Culturally Responsive Districts and Schools* is driven by a leap of faith that when educators have the knowledge, processes, and tools in hand, they will move forward in doing right by our most marginalized children, families, and communities. This application guide is also inspired by the many ways we have seen educators, families, and youth in districts and schools utilize the processes and tools in this book to shift their systems.

Through our partnership with many districts, we have learned that the process and tools in this book are useful to shift beliefs, policies, practices, and procedures only when they *do not* take shortcuts and make a long-term commitment to the journey. To that end, it is *not* about seeking quick fixes to a very complex historical education issue; instead, it requires being brave to engage in difficult conversations about race and racism and acknowledging how it operates in schools. It further warrants understanding the purpose of the work, developing a clear moral imperative of the importance of the work, communicating it to multiple stakeholders, and existing in bravery and conviction around the importance of the work, especially when opponents of the work resist or attempt to end it. It also requires centering, involving, listening to, and believing children, families, communities, and educators who are harmed and most impacted. That is, if you fail to engage the stakeholders most impacted and continue to move with the status quo, you will continue to cause harm and exclusion. Once you know that harm has been caused, and continue to do the same, you are culpable. Finally, this work requires challenging beliefs that disproportionality is not a child issue; it is an adult and systems issue.

The journey of dismantling disproportionality is both challenging and rewarding. As you read through this preface, know that there are others who have been where you are now; know that there are educators, parents/caregivers, and young people who are ready to join you; and know that when you are doing right by our children in offering them a truly just schooling experience, that is the reward.

Start your journey today and know that you will and can change your district and school!

Acknowledgments

We are forever grateful to the leaders and educators who trusted us over multiple years to partner alongside them to engage in the process and tools we discuss in this book. We learned with them and through them how to tailor our evidence-based approach to be responsive to their needs and the usefulness of our process that led to change in districts. For many of our young people who engaged in and led the Youth Center for Disproportionality (YCfD), you remain our inspiration and guiding light on why we show up. For the families we met in districts, we thank you for always being an advocate for our children and for being brave when others have not been.

We are thankful to the mentors and scholars who have come before us and built the foundation of our work. We want to thank Dr. Eddie Fergus, who has been a mentor to the first author and a visionary in developing system-based solutions to address disproportionality. We have learned so much from the transformative work they have done in districts, and the processes and tools they have developed and implemented that have left an imprint on how to engage the work. This guide has been inspired by their work. We are thankful to Dr. Pedro Noguera, who has dedicated their career to advocating for our most marginalized children. They are a constant reminder that we cannot engage in technical work without engaging in the adaptive work. We continue to be inspired by the many scholars whom we build our work from and who continue to push us to challenge the status quo: Dr. Gloria Ladson-Billings, Dr. Geneva Gay, Dr. Beth Harry, Dr. Russell Skiba, Dan Losen, Dr. Aydin Bal, Dr. Anne Gregory, Dr. Django Paris, Dr. Wendy Cavendish, Dr. Margaret Beale-Spencer, Dr. Beverly Tatum, and Dr. Bettina Love.

We continued to be in awe of Dr. Alfredo J. Artiles, who has continued to offer mentorship, support, guidance, and belief in our work. Their authenticity and mentorship has had a tremendous impact. We are grateful for Brian Ellerbeck for the ongoing support, guidance, patience, encouragement, and honesty as we have moved through this book. We are grateful for all our friends, educators, and colleagues who have reviewed our work to make this book better. This book cannot be what it is without your careful reading and feedback.

We want to thank the state where CfD resided for reimagining how disproportionality for students with an IEP by race/ethnicity can be tackled. The work of CfD would not have been possible without their support. We are grateful for the districts and organizations who have demonstrated their commitment to the work through their multiyear partnership with the Center for Systemic Change (CSC).

We are thankful to many of the directors and associates who were part of CfD and CSC and their commitment to developing and implementing a courageous scope of work to change the conditions and experiences for students of color (in particular, Black, Latinx, and Indigenous/Native), students with an IEP, and multilingual learners and students holding these intersecting identities. We are thankful to Dr. Patrick Jean-Pierre for modeling a courageous, authentic, and transformative approach to implementing the work. We are thankful to David Lopez, co-author of *Dismantling Disproportionality,* who was deeply influential in innovating CfD's content and delivery and continues to be a leading voice in this work. We are thankful to the third author, Dr. Hui-Ling S. Malone, for her vision to engage our young people who are impacted in schooling and to ensure their voice was grounded in our work. We also want to thank and acknowledge the work of the current team at CSC. Dr. Andolyn Brown's deep expertise continues to push the current iteration of our work. Demiana Rizkalla's youth leadership has been there from the start.

Finally, the first and second authors want to thank our families for their ongoing support for allowing us to leave our homes to pursue our life passion and for still holding space for us to share our experiences in the field. Thank you for your grace and empathetic listening.

Dismantling Disproportionality in Practice

CHAPTER 1

Introduction

> To any citizen of this country who figures himself as responsible—and particularly those of you who deal with the minds and hearts of young people—must be prepared to "go for broke." Or to put it another way, you must understand that in the attempt to correct so many generations of bad faith and cruelty, when it is operating not only in the classroom but in society, you will meet the most fantastic, the most brutal, and then most determined resistance. There is no point in pretending that this won't happen.
>
> —James Baldwin (1963), "A Talk to Teachers"

Are we prepared to "go for broke?" And if so, what is our path forward? In *Dismantling Disproportionality: A Culturally Responsive and Sustaining Systems Approach*, authors Hernández, Lopez, and Swier (2023) outline the importance of interrogating both bias-based beliefs and the systems they maintain in order to disrupt and dismantle the inequities that exist in our schools. From challenging color-evasiveness (failure to be race-conscious) to inept leadership messaging and toothless policy implementation, there are many roadblocks to achieving a more equity-driven school system. That said, the authors highlight a path forward. Culturally responsive and sustaining education (CR-SE) becomes "a way of being," steeped in beliefs, policies, procedures, and practices—*a way of being* that cultivates an environment where every student and family is welcomed and affirmed and provided an academic pathway that challenges and meets their needs. A culturally responsive environment also meets and sustains the needs of our educators in their everyday work. This application guide further outlines that path, supported by a theory of change (see Figure 1.1) that brings individuals and systems from awareness to understanding to practices and inevitably to sustained behaviors. Through a deep connection to both the technical and the adaptive work, educators and the schools we work in can and must create environments where CR-SE is the foundation and not just another surface-level initiative.

This application guide offers tangible next steps—tools, protocols, and processes—that call us in to do the work of both interrogating current

Figure 1.1. Theory of Change

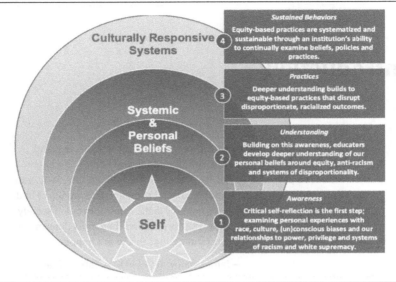

gaps and outlining steps toward more equity-responsive environments. The tools that are offered in this book are grown from almost 20 years of research and practice in the field. Each component has been built, adapted, and implemented by some of the country's leading education reformers and activists, and have effectively served in both uprooting disproportionate student outcomes and experiences in districts and outlining the steps forward. The tools, protocols, and processes have been used by in-district educators across the country and by high school student activists as well!

For those new to this work, we want to again name how we examine the cultural responsiveness of our schools. Understanding how disproportionality impacts school outcomes and experiences allows educators to identify the root causes for inequities in classrooms and school systems. As a state technical assistance provider for 15 years, we bring an application of federal policy with us in our work as we analyze disproportionality (i.e., disproportionality guidelines initiated through the Individuals with Disabilities Education Act). The U.S. Department of Education highlights disproportionality as a double-edged sword, underscored by the overrepresentation of a specific group in special education programs or disciplinary outcomes *and/or* the underrepresentation of a specific group in accessing intervention services, resources, programs, and rigorous curriculum. That said, the definition of disproportionality that was created by young folks who were a part of our Youth Center for Disproportionality (YCfD; more on YCfD in Chapter 5) has been our guiding light and critical to how we have pushed to center the voices and experiences of those most impacted. Their definition is:

> *Disproportionality is the outcome of institutionalized racism and bias that result in discriminatory beliefs, policies, and practices that negatively affect historically marginalized groups in contrast to privileged groups.*

Our young people push us to tackle the "why?"—to dive deeper than simple outcomes and to urge individuals and systems to look at root causes in order to build a better path forward.

Those most impacted by disproportionality and inequitable schooling experiences will continually highlight that one of the main reasons so many schooling spaces haven't moved or become more equitable is because the voices and experiences that matter the most are not offered a seat at the table. The most effective school-based change is led by and with the voices of those most impacted, which historically has been our Black and Indigenous/Native students, and other students of color; students with an IEP; multilingual learners; as well as students who hold other intersecting marginalized identities (e.g., LGTBQIA+, students from low-income families). As we move through processes and tools for change, we must never forget to ask the question, *What voices and experiences need to be central to this work? How do we create an environment primed for change through a continuous feedback loop with students and families?* School reform efforts more often than not miss this step from the very beginning. It doesn't matter what tool or process you follow if the folks most integral to the work are not included in some substantial way—attempts at equity shifts will continue to fail. Furthermore, effective technical assistance and training must be inquiry-based and co-created with local communities (Hernández et al., 2023; Kozleski & Artiles, 2012). In our first book, we offered the intersecting frameworks of *Improvement Science* (Jackson et al., 2018), *Essential Supports for School Improvement* (Bryk et al., 2010), and *Coherence* (Fullan & Quinn, 2016) as guiding steps that, when grounded in CR-SE, shift student experiences and outcomes. We contend, and will push further in this guide, that these methods of improvement and change can't be implemented *to* people and communities, but rather must be implemented *with* people and communities.

Grounded by a culturally responsive, critically conscious lens, these frameworks offer the bird's-eye view that is essential to shifts in policies and practices in schools. Improvement science (Jackson et al., 2018) continues to acknowledge the multiyear investment necessary for systems change work, guided by an active and ongoing analysis of data (both quantitative and qualitative). These data must focus on those most impacted and include a feedback loop to continually bring this voice and experience front and center. The Essential Supports for School Improvement (Bryk et al., 2010) recognizes the impact school and district leaders have on any potential change in a district's approach to culturally responsive practices. We intersect this with a Coherence framing—coherence in district messaging around the importance of equity work, creating a collaborative culture to implement the work, and coherence in the accountability structures needed to activate and sustain necessary change (Fullan & Quinn, 2016). Our theory of change has continued to be refined and strengthened as we work with new districts across the country and as we recognize new and old challenges that continue to impact progress.

THE STATE OF THE WORK

We recently led the first of six sessions of CR-SE training with an almost entirely white participant group, in a small suburban district. Our first session of the series is grounded in building awareness, shared language, and CR-SE concepts that may be new to many participants. In overwhelmingly white groups, we purposely open with a space to introduce language, words like Latinx, Black and/or African American, Indigenous, and also white. While moving through the *Defining Terms* learning process, participants shared their discomfort with not knowing—not knowing how to refer to "others" and not feeling comfortable naming race. One white prekindergarten teacher was visibly struggling: face caught in a frown, deep in tangled thought, clearly questioning how to engage students and the world around them. Once the group debriefed this process, she finally remarked, "If we are trying to treat everyone equally, aren't we making it worse to separate people by race?" This seemed to open a valve that others were waiting for. Another teacher exclaimed, "We keep talking about it [referring to race] and it seems like it hasn't made anything better." One of the facilitators then scrolled back to the document where participants were asked to identify if the terms being discussed were talked about in their childhood and personal lives. Almost exclusively, each group wrote, "No, not talked about" or "Not much." The facilitator then asked the group, "Have we talked about race enough?" The group went on to discuss the importance of naming identities and systems that continue to impact the well-being of our students. Without recognizing the inequitable outcomes as a result of systemic racism, we will only continue to reinforce harm.

This example highlights a common theme we see across districts throughout the country: a visceral discomfort, approaching fear, of not knowing what to say—an overwhelming lack of "racial stamina" (DiAngelo, 2018) that inevitably leads to the perpetuation of the status quo. In a U.S. context, a deeply inequitable school system has been the norm, which is counter to the message we often receive of education as the *great equalizer*. Our K–12 school system has mirrored the anti-Black racism historically grounding every institution in the country (Spencer & Ullucci, 2023). From this origin, the institution of public education has particularly been focused on perpetuating a culture devoted to whiteness (Odom Pough, 2021).

An important auxiliary to the example above are the participants who have developed some awareness and shared language—often the white progressives who read an article or two and listen to the newest NPR podcasts, for example. The most distinct barrier with this group, however, becomes the insistence on receiving the strategies to just "get the work done"—less of an interrogation of self and more of a blaming of a system and then an obfuscation of personal responsibility by way of expressing a desire for someone to just tell them what to do (Pollock et al., 2010). It is critical that we highlight this particular reality because books like the one we are offering—steeped in tangible takeaways and practice-based steps—will not move systems if readers and educators do not continually engage their own critical self-reflection and accountability (Khalifa, 2018). We cannot move through a school year implementing policies without reckoning with the personal growth needed to uphold said policies. Moreover, we cannot dismantle the racial disproportionality that lives within beliefs, policies, procedures, and practices (BPPPs) without starting with self (Hernández et al., 2023).

SO WHAT CAN THIS ACTIVE EQUITY WORK LOOK LIKE?

Gloria Ladson-Billings (1995) called for education that leads to growing a critical consciousness for every child. Gholdy Muhammad (2020) grounds the work of schooling through sharpening our students' criticality—developing the ability to read texts to understand power, authority, and oppression. Gholdy Muhammad, Bettina Love, and Dena Simmons, among others, also highlight Black joy and Black genius rather than the age-old tropes of plight and struggle educators often lean on when looking to center our Black and Brown students. These foundational approaches are happening in spaces across the country—led primarily by people of color, but also in spaces that are multiracial or even predominantly white.

In all cases, the work becomes a continuous interrogation and reflection of self and a continual connection to systems and structures that uphold BPPPs that impact all stakeholders in a school building. The active work within this space is then highlighting and moving with (not away from) the tensions that inevitably arise while doing anti-racist, equity work (Pollock et al., 2010).

In one of our districts there is a group of about 25 educators, all previously trained in the six-session CR-SE series, who have come together for a new district-wide learning space called *CR-SE in Action*. A handful of these educators have also taken on the role of district co-facilitator, training other educators in the CR-SE series. These educators have recognized that the work is never-ending and the resistance to it isn't going anywhere. This group was actively looking for a community of support within a district and surrounding community that continues to value and uphold white normative culture in both school procedures and practices. Amidst pushback from many families caught up in the fearmongering and misinformation around equity and anti-racist work, their district also committed to a multiyear implementation plan to train every educator in CR-SE. The learning in this new *CR-SE in Action* space didn't start with *"Can we stop talking about race?"* but rather was led by inquiry-based questions using an intersectional lens, starting with self and connecting to systems—specifically, thinking about how they can more effectively create schooling conditions that are welcoming and affirming for every student. They started with questions like this one:

> I see in our climate survey data that Black students were the least likely to say that they feel a connection to a teacher they can trust. How can we implement a practice that builds relationships and leaves our students feeling more deeply seen?

This group then moved with this throughline to develop continuous improvement (Jackson et al., 2018) plans, through their particular roles and focus areas, to hopefully shift the outcomes and experiences they are actively analyzing. These learning spaces are grounded in what Gorski et al. (2022) call the *Equity Imperative Leap*, where culturally responsive, anti-racist, equity work is not an option—it is the only way forward.

MOVING SYSTEMS

The example above highlights both personal and system commitments. There is the work of our individual educators who see CR-SE as part of their moral imperative and, most simply, as *good teaching*. There is then the district's commitment to providing training and support and forging sustainable, foundational pathways for continued equity work—districts that see equity as central to educational excellence. Conversely, so many of our districts and schools have relied on "initiatives" or particular individuals to own and maintain the work of moving toward equitable experiences for our children (Fullan & Quinn, 2016). In the past 3 years, particularly in the wake of the murder of George Floyd, we have seen district leaders take a myriad of approaches to the national call for a "racial reckoning." It has been overwhelmingly clear that districts that simply updated a mission statement with vague language about diversity, inclusion, and equity (DEI), or at most hired a DEI coordinator and subsequently thrust any and all things DEI related upon them, are deeply struggling to shift school cultures and systems that are still anti-Black, still exclusionary, still harmful. Django Paris (2019) writes,

> "Diversity" and "inclusion" may be the subtlest, and so in some ways the most dangerous, in their centering of whiteness. The terms are used to name students ("diverse students") and processes of assimilation (inclusion into what?) often without naming race and other intersecting and crucial memberships (e.g., gender, sexuality, dis/ability, language) or the ways educational settings (and studies of such settings) position those memberships. (p. 219).

Engagement in this work looks much different than surface-level attempts at DEI.

In our first book we offered district patterns of resistance and engagement—how districts fall within the readiness parameters of entry point, midpoint, or endpoint. As we think about systemic change, sustainably shifting cultures that have been embedded in our nation's schools for decades, it is important to think about the markers in Table 1.1 that highlight where a district needs to be to optimize success.

SETTING THE TABLE FOR SYSTEMS WORK: PROCESSES FOR CR-SE ENGAGEMENT

Schools that are culturally responsive and sustaining become spaces of institutional self-reflection (Khalifa, 2018). To do so, there are distinct interventions and learning processes educators must employ to build a system that is embedded with this continual reflection. In doing this work in schools in the past decade, it is readily apparent that critical self-reflection is not something educators can just call upon if they have never intentionally made space for the practice. In all of our trainings, we spend significant

Table 1.1. District Patterns of Resistance and Engagement

Endpoint	Overall	• Long-term commitment to the work • Development of long-term plans • Data systems to consistently monitor disproportionality • Assign staff/leader to direct the work or create a position for CRE/equity coordinator
	Logistics	• Commitment to ongoing training • Allocation of resources (e.g., time, substitutes for teachers) • Scheduling of work ahead of time
	Buy-in	• Identified participants attend the majority of the training/TA sessions • District leader and other staff are championing the work
	Dissemination and Follow-Through	• Messaging of work • Turnkeying the work • Implementing a train-the-trainer model
	Attitudes and Beliefs	• Views CRE training as foundation to work • Acknowledging disproportionality • Engaging race discussions

time building participants' stamina for self-reflection. We deepen the understanding of the ways in which power and privilege (that live in particular identities—cisgendered, male, white, affluent, nondisabled—and within institutions) impact the ability to create welcoming and affirming school spaces for historically and currently marginalized identities. Three key learning processes we engage in every session (regardless of length) are:

- Developing and maintaining a contract for the group,
- Outlining and discussing racial equity tensions (Pollock et al., 2010), and
- Practicing naming and discussing the elephants in the room.

In an effort to recognize why these three pieces are critical and to share our own best practices that you will hopefully use in your own communities (during staff meetings, professional learning communities, etc.), we are outlining each of the processes and offering essential questions as you look to push your own development and that of your school or district.

DEVELOPING A CONTRACT

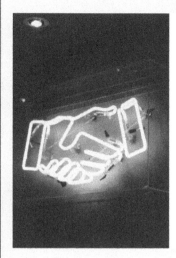

NYU | STEINHARDT

Contract

+Listen with respect
+Struggle together
+Participate and remain engaged
+Push your growing edge
+Consider what's in it for me
+Expect to experience discomfort
+Speak your truth and keep it real
+Try not to take it personally
+Intent vs. Impact
+Confidentiality

"As we struggle together, we will have hit the growing edge — push your growing edge!

The People's Institute for Survival and Beyond

- The items listed in a group's contract become the norms of operating, the values that drive the work. White normative spaces purposefully avoid (consciously and unconsciously) many of the pieces listed in the contract we use (image above).
- Without struggle there will be no change. The work of CR-SE is inherently moving in opposition to systems of power and privilege that continue to be upheld in schools.
- One of the biggest hurdles to deeper self-reflection lives in the ways in which educators default to *intent* and fail to focus on *impact*. Teachers, by and large, are in schools with the best intentions, yet anti-Blackness and transphobia continue to harm students every day. We must move to thinking about how we are impacting communities rather than just living in our intent.
- Contracts must be co-created and malleable and adapt to what and how the community is feeling. This can change within a session or meeting. Make space to explicitly ask, "What contract pieces are important to us today?"

Essential Questions as You Engage in Your Own Contract Development:

- How are you "setting the table" for deep reflection and difficult, often messy dialogue?
- In what spaces are you establishing norms like these?

- Are you doing this with students, and are you listening to what they need and adapting to those needs as the year progresses?

Action Steps:

- Have the dialogue with young people. Ask your students what they need to foster a space of criticality and consciousness-raising. The responses from young people should drive the contract development for adult and youth learning spaces.
- Using the above contract as a guide, move into your next meeting and ask what contract norms the group needs to center equity in the conversation.

RACIAL EQUITY TENSIONS

NYU STEINHARDT

WHAT CAN I DO?

Each practitioner routinely questions their own personal readiness to become the type of professional who can successfully engage issues of race and racism in their life and classroom practice.

PERSONAL

WHAT CAN I DO?

Practitioners routinely question the power of the individual educator to counteract structural or societal problems of racial and race-class inequality via the classroom.

STRUCTURAL

WHAT CAN I DO?

Practitioners routinely search for concrete actionable steps they can take in their classrooms and schools, questioning how abstract ideas of theories about racial inequality and difference can help them.

STRATEGIES

- Educators must move **with** the three identified tensions when directly engaging racial equity work (Pollock et al., 2010). Our ability to directly engage these tensions has a direct connection to our ability to shift practices and systems.
- It is important to name these tensions, not allowing them to become a barrier to doing the work, but to actively acknowledge how they are a part of the journey forward.
- Often, all three tensions arise simultaneously as educators look to respond to root-cause inequities.

Personal

- This tension focuses on an educator's individual readiness to engage critical equity issues.
- What parts of my own identity do I need to continue to reflect upon to be able to effectively move with the personal tension?
- For example: *How can I as a white, nondisabled, cisgendered male effectively address inequities that come up in my classroom?*

Structural

- Educators face countless societal forces, expectations, and messages every day, even before walking into the classroom. Examples include the tension of not having enough time or decision-making power over curriculum—tensions that continue to impact necessary equity pushes.
- Another structural example is the misinformation around Critical Race Theory that has been used as a fearmongering tactic to push educators to not engage in race conversations—it is a structural force that many educators feel.

Strategy

- There is no silver bullet in inquiry-based equity work. Unfortunately, there is also no checklist to immediately dismantle disproportionality.
- Educators do, however, have to make space for the everyday and long-term strategies that do exist and be open to what colleagues of color and young folks are sharing in order to implement different practices.

Essential Questions as You Engage the Racial Equity Tensions:

- How can you make sure you (and your community) are moving **with** the tensions and not away from them?
- How can this language/concept acquisition create more comfort in the discomfort and facilitate diving deeper into responding to the root causes for existing inequities?
- Are you transparently leading with your own personal identities as you reflect in your own readiness? Are you modeling this for others?

Action Steps:

- **Read** the article *"But what can I do?": Three Necessary Tensions in Teaching Teachers About Race* (Pollock et al., 2010).

- Dialogue and outline how the three tensions exist in your learning community. Make sure the conversation is race-conscious and focused on the intersectional identities that impact creating culturally responsive spaces. Practice *Naming the Elephants in the Room* (outlined below) while you have your dialogue.

NAMING THE ELEPHANTS IN THE ROOM

NYU STEINHARDT

Process: Discussing the Elephant in the Room

Our educational systems have disproportionately negative impacts on particular groups of students:

+Children of color (particularly Black, Indigenous and Latinx children)
+Boys of color
+Black girls
+Children of low socio-economic backgrounds
+LGBTQIA+ students
+Gender nonconforming students
+Children with an Individualized Education Plan (IEP)
+Families and Communities of Color

"I'm right there in the room, and no one even acknowledges me."

Elephants in the Room

- If educators are not naming who is most impacted by white supremacy and a schooling institution that still values whiteness as an operating norm, we will never reach equity. And this must include naming intersectional identities—e.g., gender, sexuality, ability, socioeconomic status—that continue to negatively impact children and families.
- *Naming the elephants in the room* becomes the first step for individuals and communities that have largely lived lives that have been deemed normative—lives of privilege. Bettina Love (Love & Sealy-Ruiz, 2019) urges folks to "take a risk, put something on the line," and this process is often the first point

of activation to name who is impacted. That said, Black folks, people of color, and trans folks have never been given the choice to discuss or not discuss, name or not name, and it is exceedingly important to center this contrasting reality.

- The individuals and communities listed in the figure above have historically, and currently, been disproportionately impacted by our school system. For each community, there is an extensive research base outlining this disproportionate impact. Moreover, if white people, specifically, take the time to just listen and *believe* the communities listed, we could avoid so much of the equity detours that result in arguing who is oppressed and who is not—which is also a manifestation of white supremacy.
- This process also asks educators to be as specific as possible— not live in coded language that often sounds like "those people" or "these kids"—to move toward equity, we must interrogate who we are actually talking about, holding biases for, and continuing to harm!

Essential Questions as You Engage in Naming the Elephants in the Room:

- Who is most impacted by academic and behavioral trajectories in your school district? In your school?
- What are young people saying? Particularly communities who hold identities that have been marginalized by society and school?
- What does your school and district data say?
- If you are having tensions about the communities listed, what learning do you need to engage in yourself to become better informed? Google (and your local library) is your friend.

Action Steps:

- Take a look at your school/district's disaggregated behavior and academic data (i.e., data that show outcomes across different identity markers like race, gender, and IEP status). Have a dialogue with staff members that focuses on naming the elephants in the room using the data that are available.
- After identifying who is impacted the most and practicing the work of naming, create a list of supports that are currently in place for said communities. What needs to be created to address the gaps?

WHAT TO EXPECT IN THE PROCEEDING CHAPTERS

As we move into the rest of this guide, the following chapters will offer a pathway for active implementation, from self to system, one that is accessible to any district/education institution across the country. We continue in Chapter 2 with a deeper dive into CR-SE, its origins, and then, more tangibly, a look at guided questions and tools educators can use to move toward a more equity-driven practice. In Chapter 3 we will outline our equity audit, or root cause analysis process, which becomes fundamental for districts to move through to more deeply understand where their specific equity gaps live and, more importantly, chart a more equitable path forward. Chapter 4 will build on the root cause process with the tools and learning exercises educators can take on themselves. Moreover, Chapters 3 and 4 are set up to scaffold understanding (Chapter 3) and then implementation (Chapter 4) of a root cause analysis process and the action planning that needs to come from it. In Chapter 5 we come back to what should always be the North Star—our young people—with an in-depth guide to developing youth-led, school-based equity work. We hope to leave you in a place of active implementation, ongoing inquiry, and excitement for the everyday work, the CR-SE journey that isn't about the final destination but about carving out a more liberating future for every child.

CHAPTER 2

Authentic CR-SE

Tackling Beliefs Through Self to System Reflection and Action

WHY CULTURALLY RESPONSIVE AND SUSTAINING EDUCATION (CR-SE)?

In our work with partnering school districts, often one of our first requests is to hear directly from students and families in the community, particularly those who have been historically and currently marginalized. To center these voices, we carry out focus groups and listening sessions. In one of these recent sessions, when asked what the barriers to equity have been in their school, one high school student shared:

> You can tell an educator, "Hey, I want you to do a unit on social injustice, and I want you to talk about these different events in recent history" and there's a lot of teachers that will say I'm not comfortable with that. You know, because unfortunately we don't have a lot of educators of color. And so that may be something that is very foreign to them, and so they want to stick to what they know. They're going to teach the history that they were taught when they were students. So the cycle continues.

Our young people have been telling us why we need a more culturally responsive approach to schooling for quite some time now. So have our community members, whose voices and expertise are continually overlooked. One community member offered their perspective on the barrier to equity and cultural responsiveness that currently exists in schools:

> We are dealing with a shortage of educators that are able to comprehensively take that information from theory and demonstrate what that looks like in application and how that translates into what's happening today, you know. What we're seeing now is we have large groups of people still walking around saying they don't believe that discrimination still exists. They don't

believe that the deck is stacked against people of color. They don't believe that white privilege is [a] thing and this is because you know the information is not being taught correctly in the school.

These perspectives have been echoed across the country by dozens of other students and community members we have heard from as we have engaged in this work.

With student voice and student experience as our charge, we ask educators to move through this chapter, broadening both personal awareness and understanding of cultural responsiveness, while also using the tools we offer to actualize tangible next steps to building more culturally responsive school environments. In this chapter we discuss culturally responsive and sustaining education (CR-SE) and outline ways educators, districts, and schools can develop competency and capacity to grow the work of CR-SE at a personal and systemic level. In order to understand CR-SE, we must first address how race is embedded in schooling structures through a critical race perspective. Critical Race Theory (CRT) sheds light on the urgency of understanding culturally relevant pedagogy (CRP) and culturally sustaining pedagogies (CSP-HM) and their specific tenets. Furthermore, and at the core, we address the connections between CRT and CR-SE to more deeply understand where we need to go with this work. It is important to interrogate personal values and beliefs, particularly through the lens of some of the most influential voices who for decades have fought for more inclusive, justice-driven schools. We will examine Critical Race Theory, CRP, and CSP to ultimately lead into the work of interrogating personal beliefs and practices in pursuit of systemic change.

This chapter is positioned to support education practitioners to engage both theory and practice in the effort to enact positive change within schooling systems. Throughout the chapter, we offer application exercises that have been used with the Center for Disproportionality's (CfD) many partnering districts. These exercises are built from an understanding of what it takes to specifically engage everyday anti-racism and cultural responsiveness from the self to classrooms and within schools and districts. Furthermore, each learning exercise also positions both self and system as focus areas. We ask readers to continue to think about the following questions:

- What can I learn about myself as I move through these exercises that will further support how I engage my students, particularly those who hold identities different from my own?
- How will each application exercise move me/us as a school/ district to create more culturally responsive learning

environments for historically and currently marginalized students, staff, and families?

FOUNDATIONAL UNDERSTANDINGS (PRECONDITIONS) CRITICAL TO CR-SE AND SELF TO SYSTEM WORK

Critical Race Theory in Education

Before we launch into the difficult work of examining personal beliefs and practices, we find it necessary to examine *systems* that are fraught with racism and injustice. A helpful way to unmask race and power within institutions, and as this book concerns, educational institutions, we look through the perspective of Critical Race Theory (CRT). In recent years, CRT has been a source of panic and vitriol, particularly among the political right. According to the UCLA School of Law Critical Race Studies Program (2023), "Since September 2020, a total of 183 local, state, and federal government entities across the United States have introduced 521 anti–Critical Race Theory bills, resolutions, executive orders, opinion letters, statements, and other measures" (p. 1). CRT is not synonymous with culturally relevant or sustaining pedagogies, yet they are not entirely exclusive; therefore it is important to understand CRT in the conversation around anti-racist education and CR-SE.

What Is CRT and Why Does It Matter?

CRT was born out of critical legal studies to examine how legal systems maintain hegemony and inequality. Yet, since critical legal studies did not specifically address race, legal scholars of the 1970s and 1980s such as Derrick Bell, Mari Matsuda, Richard Delgado, and Kimberlé Crenshaw conceptualized what we now know as Critical Race Theory. After the Civil Rights Movement and significant legislation was passed to support the advancement of Black people and other people of color in America, unfortunately the pervasive problem of racism was not solved. For instance, after *Brown v. Board of Education*, and schools were desegregated, Black students continued to have inferior education and white students continued to segregate themselves through racist systems of tracking and other gatekeeping to exclude Black students from accessing their classrooms (Lucas & Berends, 2002). As of today, schools are still very much segregated, with white students the most segregated demographic in the nation (Frankenberg et al., 2019).

Instead of becoming colorblind, or more accurately, *color-evasive*, CRT is an ideology and academic and legal framework that considers racism as a normal and permanent fixture in American life (Bell, 2008). A CRT lens unmasks and exposes racism as embedded in laws, policies, and institutions instead of viewing racism as a result of individual bias and prejudice (NAACP Legal Defense Fund, 2023).

In 1995, Ladson-Billings and Tate wrote the article "Toward a Critical Race Theory of Education" to bring the conversation of CRT into education. They highlighted that "school desegregation has meant increased white flight along with a loss of African-American teaching and administrative positions" (p. 56) and that desegregation continued to benefit white people. They developed three propositions: (1) race continues to be a significant factor in determining inequity in the United States, (2) U.S. society is based on property rights,[1] and (3) the intersection of race and property creates an analytic tool through which we can understand social (and, consequently, school) inequity. As Ladson-Billings and Tate mention, the focus on race does not take away from gender or class oppression, but it is necessary to understand why Black and Latinx students are disciplined disproportionately and not seen as academically successful. This brings in the conversation of race as property[2] (Harris, 1993) and how this was and continues to be prevalent in our schools. Gloria Ladson-Billings extended the scholarship around CRT in education with her 1998 piece, "Just What Is Critical Race Theory and What's It Doing in a Nice Field Like Education?" Because CRT was still rarely applied in conversation among educators such as teachers, education policymakers, administrators, and so forth, she brought CRT to the fore. Complete Table 2.1 (below), which addresses how Ladson-Billings viewed education from a CRT lens and provides space for you to identify where race and racism lives within your schooling context.

Now that we have identified where race and racism exist within schooling structures (curriculum, instruction, assessment, funding, etc.), we turn to culturally relevant and sustaining pedagogies as a medium to disrupt racism and the beliefs and practices that harm children of color.

Origins and Tenets of CR-SE: Culturally Relevant and Sustaining Pedagogies

In Gloria Ladson-Billings's recent book, *Culturally Relevant Pedagogy: Asking A Different Question*, she writes, "Perhaps the most 'radical' thing I have done in my work is to ask a different question. Instead of scratching my head and joining the chorus of voices that asked what was wrong with Black children, I dared to ask, 'What is *right* with Black students and what happens in classrooms where teachers, parents, and students get it right?'" (Ladson-Billings, 2021, p. 2). This question is the heart of

Table 2.1. Through a Critical Race Theory Lens, Where Do Race and Racism Live in Schools?

Facet of Schooling	CRT Lens	Example	Your example of how race and racism live in this facet of schooling
Curriculum	"a culturally specific artifact designed to maintain a white supremacist master script" (Ladson-Billings, 1998, p. 18).	Misrepresenting or complete erasure of Black historical figures, like "we are all immigrants" who went through Ellis Island or that Rosa Parks was just a tired seamstress instead of a longtime activist who deliberately resisted white power.	
Instruction	"suggests that current instructional strategies presume that African American students are deficient" (Ladson-Billings, 1998, p. 19).	Instruction does not take into account cultural ways of knowing and being, and that instruction is generic that works for all students.	
Assessment	Derived from intelligence testing that legitimizes that Black students are inferior under the guise of "scientific rationalism."	High-stakes testing that stem from eugenics. Assessment measures "may tell us that students do not know what is on the test, but fail to tell us what students actually know and are able to do" (Ladson-Billings, 1998, p. 20).	
School Funding	Predominately white and affluent areas receive more funding and resources than Black and Brown working-class areas.	The viral TikTok video of Carmel High School displaying elaborate wealth and resources.	
Where else does racism live in your school/ district?			

CR-SE—it is looking for the strengths of all students, instead of depending on systems that create standards of "normalcy" that are embedded with whiteness.

Ladson-Billings coined the term *culturally relevant pedagogy* (CRP) after her seminal study conducted in the 1990s regarding the effective teaching of Black students. She noted that previous research on the teaching of Black students portrayed Black youth as deficient and ignored their distinct, unique cultures and histories. Ladson-Billings defied the white gaze[3] and set out to understand what teaching, learning, and pedagogical practices nurture and uplift Black students in the classroom (Ladson-Billings, 1995). From her research, Ladson-Billings reached the definition of culturally relevant pedagogy as:

> a pedagogy of opposition not unlike critical pedagogy but specifically committed to collective, not merely individual, empowerment. Culturally relevant pedagogy rests on three criteria or propositions: (a) Students must experience **academic success**; (b) students must develop and/or maintain **cultural competence**; and (c) students must develop a **critical consciousness** through which they challenge the status quo of the current social order. (Ladson-Billings, 1995, p. 160)

Academic success meant that all students "need literacy, numeracy, technological, social, and political skills in order to be active participants in a democracy" (Ladson-Billings, 1995, p. 160) and Ladson-Billings maintained that students needed academic excellence as a foundation. Later, Ladson-Billings clarified that academic success is not to be confused with achievement on high-stakes testing, and felt that the better term was *student learning* (Ladson-Billings, 2021). **Cultural competence** meant that students could be themselves, without being punished, such as bringing in their favorite musical lyrics and speaking in their home languages. **Critical consciousness** stems from Freire's concept of *conscientizacão*, where students are given the opportunity to question the world around them instead of top-down "banking methods" of teaching. Furthermore, CRP stresses the importance of community and collective uplift that defies Eurocentric norms of individualism. Ladson-Billings wrote,

> Beyond those individual characteristics of academic achievement and cultural competence, students must develop a broader sociopolitical consciousness that allows them to critique the cultural norms, values, mores, and institutions that produce and maintain social inequities. If school is about preparing students for active citizenship, what better citizenship tool than the ability to critically analyze the society? (Ladson-Billings, 1995, p. 162)

CRP interrupts cultural erasure and positions the specific cultural knowledge and ways of existing for Black, Indigenous, and people of color (BIPOC) students as a *strength*. CRP is of the tradition that education is for liberation, particularly for BIPOC who have been historically marginalized.

Culturally sustaining pedagogy (CSP; Paris, 2012) draws from Ladson-Billings's culturally relevant pedagogy. In an increasingly racially, culturally, and linguistically diverse society, Django Paris questioned what the purpose of schooling is in *pluralistic* societies and offered a "needed change in stance and terminology," acknowledging that culturally "relevant" was not enough to capture the sentiment of an education that leads to greater social change within schooling and beyond (Paris, 2012). Thus, Paris proposed culturally *sustaining* pedagogies, which "seeks to perpetuate and foster—to sustain—linguistic, literate, and cultural pluralism as part of schooling for positive social transformation" (Paris & Alim, 2017). Not unlike CRP, CSP "demands a critical, emancipatory vision of schooling that redirects the focus of critique away from children (and their cultures, communities, languages, histories, etc.) and aims it squarely at the oppressive systems that frame us in every which way as marginal or deficient" (Alim et al., 2020, p. 263). CSP explicitly names whiteness as the problem and instead centers the ways of knowing and being of young people, and their communities and cultural practices.

CSP is a critical framework to sustain particularly Indigenous, Black, Latinx, Asian, and Pacific Islander communities and their intersections with gender and sexuality, dis/ability, class, language, land and more in a cis cisheteropatriachal white ableist society (Alim et al., 2020, p. 261). CSP maintains an education that is critical, joyful, and sustaining, and that strives toward equity and social justice.

CR-SE does not take on an assimilationist approach where students must change to fit into an existing social order. Instead, CRP uses students' culture to empower themselves to critically examine educational content and interrogate the role they have in creating a truly democratic society (Ladson-Billings, 1995).

How are the tenets of CRP and CSP embedded in your practices? Table 2.2 contains the key features of CRP and CSP and questions to guide you in thinking where there are gaps in actualizing CR-SE in your beliefs, policies, and practices.

Culturally relevant and sustaining classrooms provide a space for hope, possibility, radical imagination, and joy. Classrooms that are culturally relevant and sustaining must not be used as a space to assimilate the multiple identities of our youth into white cis heteronormative spaces (Paris & Alim, 2017). Classrooms that are culturally relevant and

Table 2.2. Key Features of CRP and CSP

Culturally Relevant Pedagogy (Ladson-Billings, 1995)	Culturally Sustaining Pedagogies (Paris, 2021)
• Students must experience academic success (*student learning*). • Students must develop and/or maintain cultural competence. • Students must develop a critical consciousness through which they challenge the status quo of the current social order.	• A critical centering of dynamic communities, their valued languages, practices, and knowledges across the learning setting • Student and intergenerational community agency and input, what McCarty and Lee (2014) named "community accountability," where families, elders, and students are understood as central collaborators in learning settings, offering invitations, consultations, approvals, and input. • Working to be in good relationship with the land, the people of the land, with students and communities (this means developing reciprocal relationships with Indigenous communities, the lands and places of the work, and with one another in learning settings). • Structured opportunities to contend with internalized oppressions, false choices, and inward gazes (Paris, 2021).

sustaining are *emancipatory* and recognize that literacy is an avenue to critically examine the world around us, use cultural practices as an asset and not a deficit to enrich learning, and evoke joy while transforming our society toward justice and liberation for our youth and communities.

We highlight the origins and tenets of CRT, CRP, and CSP as we move to interrogate the self in relation to CR-SE. Unfortunately, three decades after Ladson-Billings coined CRP, many classrooms have corrupted and distorted CR-SE (Paris, 2019). Instead of a critical education meant to critique and change society, mainstream educators began to conflate CRP with consuming "ethnic" foods and celebrating holidays. Applying a CRT framework helps to explain why CR-SE is important and needed in our schools. Race is embedded in the bones of schooling. To maintain teaching and learning that is color-evasive does a disservice to our students because it ignores the valued backgrounds and identities of students, marking whiteness as normal. CR-SE gives students the tools to critically examine their own lived realities and then to transform their lives to make them better for themselves, their communities, and their futures. CR-SE maintains an element of criticality, yet there is also a foundation of joy, love, and futurity (Muhammad, 2020).

Starting With Self: Bringing in the Self to Interrogate Values and Beliefs

After defining culturally responsive and sustaining pedagogies and how race and racism are central in education through the lens of Critical Race Theory, it's important to understand how these ideas live in ourselves. Understanding race intellectually or theoretically should not disconnect ourselves from our own values and beliefs that may be racist, considering that each of us is socialized in an inherently racist society (Bonilla-Silva, 2017; DiAngelo, 2018). In order to create culturally affirming spaces for our students, where they are able to grow their own critical consciousness, educators must actively process how ideologies of race and racism live in ourselves. In coming back to our theory of change (highlighted in Chapter 1), it is critical that we work to more deeply understand what it means to "Start with Self." Yolanda Sealey-Ruiz's concept of "archaeology of the self" (2019), which lies within her "racial literacy framework" (image below), further provides a framework for interrogating one's own values and beliefs.

A tension we find among teachers, leaders, and education practitioners is that they want to know *how* to do CR-SE in classrooms before understanding the *why* of these asset-based pedagogies. Those who truly practice CR-SE will tell you that CR-SE is not a set of lesson plans or

Figure 2.1. Archeology of Self

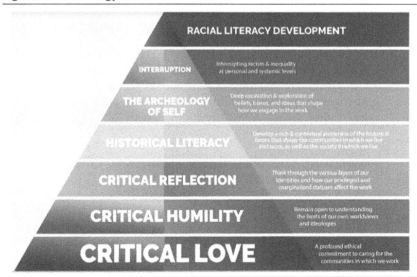

toolkits; rather, it is a *way of being*, knowing and showing up in the world (Paris & Alim, 2017). A central part is understanding how you were socialized to think about race. Understanding your own stories and traumas is necessary before entering a classroom with students, because, as Sealey-Ruiz warns us, you will cause harm. Sealey-Ruiz's concept of the archaeology of self is knowing your own story in order to be open to other people's stories. Teaching is about connection. And we connect best with others when we know ourselves. Archaeology of self is an important part of the racial literacy framework because in order to become racially literate, one must take a deep dive into their selves.

According to Sealey-Ruiz:

> Individuals who develop racial literacy are able to engage in the necessary personal reflection about their racial beliefs and practices, and teach their students to do the same. Racial literacy in schools includes the ability to read, write about, discuss and interrupt situations and events that are motivated and upheld by racial inequity and bias. Sustaining racial literacy across the lifespan is possible by engaging in an "Arch of Self"—an action-oriented process requiring love, humility, reflection, an understanding of history, and a commitment to working against racial injustice. (from https://www .yolandasealeyruiz.com/archaeology-of-self)

As Sealey-Ruiz's students put it, their archaeology of self and racial literacy journey was "a living practice of developing our own racial literacy through individual reflection and collaborative analysis" (Bell et al., 2022, p. 4). Below are resources to learn more about the archaeology of self:

- https://youtu.be/OwC_3cLRJO8?si=Je2HGxpP-k9g-1wc
- https://soundcloud.com/nychealingcollective/episode-1-healing -through-the-archaeology-of-self-with-dr-yolanda-sealey-ruiz ?utm_source=clipboard&utm_medium=text&utm_campaign =social_sharing

FROM FOUNDATIONAL UNDERSTANDINGS TO CR-SE SELF TO SYSTEM APPLICATION

In our CR-SE work with districts, this idea of "starting with self" spirals throughout the six sessions of our culturally responsive and sustaining education training series, as the work of critical self-reflection is not a feat accomplished, but a muscle grown to continually be used. There are four key learning processes that support this work and that should be engaged by all educators. The order of the learning processes is purposeful. Educators should ideally move through these in the order they are outlined as scaffolded professional development. We highlight and expand upon the four processes below for you to apply individually and in your district/school communities:

1. Defining Terms
2. Own Culture
3. Memories of Race
4. Social Identity Profile

Below you will find a description and directions for each of these learning processes. Our goal is that you both engage them individually and also become a co-facilitator in this work with colleagues. In many of our districts we have trained co-facilitators who now, years later, lead trainings with cohorts in their districts. The four processes below are curated to activate continual self reflection—they can certainly be engaged yearly or even multiple times a year. This active work becomes central to what becomes *just good teaching*.[4]

Move through the descriptions below and then utilize the directions and the handouts to engage each learning process.

Defining Terms

We opened this book with an anecdote highlighting educators grappling with how we talk about words like "race" and in turn struggling to address the impact of race and racism in the United States context. Having worked with hundreds of teams of educators, a lack of shared language becomes a clear and immediate barrier to active equity work. The *Defining Terms* exercise is not just about growing a deeper understanding of words that get thrown around social media and friend groups, but rather connecting what we have grown to understand about each of these terms based on our own background and experiences. It is critical that the focus is on how the given term elicits critical self-reflection and moves past surface-level language acquisition. We have seen countless examples of individuals weaponizing new language in effort to appear equity-driven when, in reality, they are not committed to culturally responsive practices but, instead, are maintaining systems of oppression. To move past surface-level "DEI work" and to actually shift self and systems, we must interrogate our own connection to terms and concepts embedded in equity work—*What were we taught about race growing up? By whom? What weren't we taught?* Moreover, in the absence of learning, which is commonplace for white folks and those who hold multiple privileged identities, there is still a strong message coming through that impacts how we engage students—particularly how we engage those who hold identities that are different from our own.

In this foundational exercise, facilitators often shift the terms that are used but, more often than not, use the following as starting points to engage with participants:

1. Race
2. Ethnicity
3. Dominant cultural group
4. Subordinate cultural group
5. White (*not Caucasian)
6. People of Color (and/or Black, Indigenous, and people of color)
7. Asian
8. Black and/or African American
9. Latino/a/Hispanic/Latinx
10. Indigenous/Native American
11. Class

As facilitators, we offer the directions below when moving through this process:

DIRECTIONS FOR COMPLETING *DEFINING TERMS:*

- The group will jigsaw the learning of all of the terms. Break the whole group up into smaller groups (generally 3–5 individuals). Each group is assigned 1–2 terms to engage, depending on the group size. For each term, you are asked to first "define" the term without using our friend Google (10–15 minutes).
- After each group comes up with your best attempt at a definition, move on to having a dialogue around *What you were taught* and *What you weren't taught* about each term. Within these two questions, push yourself to identify what communities you learned from (or didn't), looking at (1) family, (2) peers, (3) School, (4) community, and (5) work (30–40 minutes).
- Come back to the whole group to share what each small group came up with, what you struggled with, any patterns you notice, and/or any questions that are still lingering. As groups share, facilitators offer slides further defining the terms and providing historical framing and current implications for each term (30–45 minutes).

- See the Chapter 2 appendices, Appendix A (https://www .tcpress.com/filebin/PDFs/9780807769447_app.pdf), for the handout for groups to move through and the list of definitions we use to support the whole-group dialogue.

The *Defining Terms* learning process has an inevitable impact on participants. During the whole-group debriefs, we have heard things like "You just don't know what you don't know." This becomes a common refrain for white educators specifically, who are recognizing they had little knowledge about the given term coming into the training. In participants' self-reflection, they begin to connect their current knowledge gaps to their upbringings. Whether consciously or unconsciously, they were not taught about identities of difference, and in many cases, if there was any direct teaching, it was about avoidance, hate, and separatism. We tell participants that even the silence or avoidance that appeared in our upbringings becomes instructive and has shaped present-day interactions, relationships, and teaching!

Our Own Culture

In Zaretta Hammond's (2015) book, *Culturally Responsive Teaching & The Brain,* she asks educators to take a deeper look at how we understand our own culture and then use this deeper understanding to more effectively support and build relationships with students. She offers several guided questions for educators to engage in this pursuit. Below you can see a subset of these questions, some of which we have adapted and others that we have added. As a next-step practice, this handout can be completed by any school-based staff member looking to further understand the impact of cultural variation within a school community and how a school may or may not be culturally responsive to students and families. See the Chapter 2 appendices, Appendix C (https://www.tcpress.com/filebin/PDFs /9780807769447_app.pdf), for the *Our Own Culture* handout.

As facilitators, we offer the directions below when moving through this learning process:

DIRECTIONS FOR COMPLETING *OUR OWN CULTURE:*

- Make sure everyone has access to the *Our Own Culture* handout.
- Complete the document on your own (20–30 minutes).
- Be ready to engage with a smaller community. Count off into groups of 4–5 (depending on group size). Discuss what you

noticed about your culture and share particular responses that
stood out to you (15–20 minutes).
• Once everyone shares in the smaller community, make sure to
  discuss the question below (10 minutes).
• Share question reflections in the whole group, further discussing
  the *thinking question* below and the potential implications
  (10 minutes).

Thinking Question:

• As you unpacked your own culture, what are some of the gaps
  you may have in your own learning/experience?

In training sessions, we pair the *Our Own Culture* learning process
with examining the cultural iceberg (see Figure 2.2, adapted from Edward
T. Hall's 1976 cultural iceberg model)—looking at the three tiers of culture. Above the waterline or the tip of the iceberg, we find surface-level
culture, which is predominantly what exists in how schools enact and
understand "culture." This often looks like the once-a-year multicultural
celebrations, which on the surface level aren't inherently bad, but can often tokenize the cultural identities of students, families, and educators in
a school community. These attempted recognitions of culture also most
often fail to be woven into the yearlong curriculum and are rarely led by
the voices and experiences of the young people and families whose cultures are often minimized or silenced in schools. Just below the waterline,
we find more of the "unspoken rules" of culture that require more im-
plicit understanding. Cultural variations in concepts of time, body language, and eye contact exist at this level. Lastly, even farther below the
waterline we uncover the unconscious rules, or "hidden culture," where
we start to understand cultural variation in habits, assumptions, and
values. It is important for us to connect the ways in which our participants move through the *Our Own Culture* handout with the layers of the
cultural iceberg. *How deeply are we understanding culture in our own
lives, and how does that impact your relationships with your students and
the layers of personal culture they bring with them into the classroom?*
This learning process serves to provide educators with a better grasp of
personal culture to better understand and more authentically connect with
others. Culturally responsive education relies on authentic relationship
building, which requires the centering of marginalized cultural communities, as highlighted in Figure 2.2.

Figure 2.2. Cultural Iceberg Model (Hall, 1976)

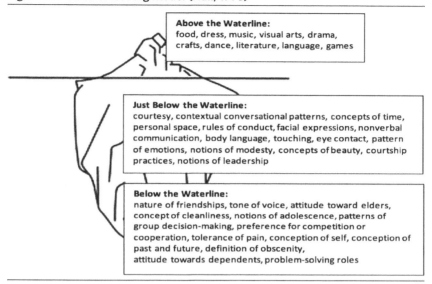

Above the Waterline:
food, dress, music, visual arts, drama, crafts, dance, literature, language, games

Just Below the Waterline:
courtesy, contextual conversational patterns, concepts of time, personal space, rules of conduct, facial expressions, nonverbal communication, body language, touching, eye contact, pattern of emotions, notions of modesty, concepts of beauty, courtship practices, notions of leadership

Below the Waterline:
nature of friendships, tone of voice, attitude toward elders, concept of cleanliness, notions of adolescence, patterns of group decision-making, preference for competition or cooperation, tolerance of pain, conception of self, conception of past and future, definition of obscenity, attitude towards dependents, problem-solving roles

Memories of Race

Countless times we have heard educators admit to us that when race is brought up in the classroom—as it relates to something being read, a lived experience, or simply an interaction between students—teachers avoid engaging the conversation and even worse, often punish students for attempting to engage in race conversations. In order to be a culturally responsive educator, we need to build both racial literacy (as noted with the archaeology of self) and further develop our racial stamina: the ability to have "race talk" (Pollock, 2004) that acknowledges the impact of race and racism in our own lives and in the lives of our students. One of the main deterrents to culturally responsive pedagogy manifests through *white fragility* (DiAngelo, 2018) and defensiveness that inevitably arises when specifically white people are confronted with conversations that center on race and racism. In a system grounded in white supremacy, white operates as raceless, while any nonwhite person is othered and negatively racialized. This also means that white educators by and large have very little racial stamina, an inability to substantively participate in conversations about race (DiAngelo, 2018). Conversely, white educators have actually developed several tools to avoid having these conversations (Picower, 2009).

The *Memories of Race* learning process centers the impact of race and racism through self-reflective writing and dialogue. In order to be culturally responsive facilitators of learning in our classrooms, we need to develop the practice of reflecting on what race has meant in our own lives.

The purpose of this learning process is to highlight both subtle and direct environmental messages that have influenced our development and the many internal biases we may hold toward ourselves and others. It

---

DIRECTIONS FOR COMPLETING *MEMORIES OF RACE:*

- Using the handout located in the Chapter 2 appendices, Appendix D (https://www.tcpress.com/filebin/PDFs/9780807769447 _app.pdf), reflect on when you were first aware of your own race.
- Create a timeline of racial experiences that contributed to shaping your awareness of your own race. Think about several events/experiences during different stages in your life that contributed to your understanding of what it means to be of a particular race as well as how you learned to perceive others who do not share the same racial background. In order to accomplish this task, follow these steps:
  1. Write about the memory of when you were first aware of your own race.
  2. Briefly describe any proceeding events and be sure to include (if possible) the approximate age you experienced it.
  3. Explain the message around race you internalized or heard from your experience. Also, indicate what emotions you had. Did you talk to anyone about it? How did you make sense of the messages you were or were not receiving?
  4. Answer the questions at the end of the handout
- Allow 30–45 minutes to complete the entire handout.
- If operating as a facilitator, be sure to emphasize the importance of being open and forthcoming and know that there are no right or wrong answers.
- After everyone has enough time to engage in the reflective writing process, move into small groups (no more than 5 people in each) to discuss takeaways and to dive deeper into the questions you answered at the end of the handout. **Note:** To mitigate potential harm, we group educators of color together in small groups. Allow up to 5 minutes per person, to share key parts of your narrative in the small group.
- Open up to the whole group for each small group to share highlights.

quickly becomes clear which educators have done some reflective work around race and which are moving through these messages and questions for the first time.

Without fail, this process elicits a lot of emotions, making it critical that there has been a dialogue around group norms before commencing this work (see "Developing a Contract" in Chapter 1). It is our practice as facilitators to also make sure this doesn't become a space where educators of color are being further harmed and invalidated by white colleagues. Grouping in racial affinity groups when possible recognizes that people of color largely share stories of personal harm when thinking of their first (and proceeding memories) of race, whereas white people share memories that aren't connected to personal harm and, in most cases, are connected to witnessing racialized harm against a person of color.

This learning process requires very thoughtful facilitation and should not be engaged without purposeful planning. That said, when executed with these parameters in mind, it can serve to powerfully give voice to the counternarratives of Black, Indigenous, and other educators of color as well as begin the process of reckoning and racial stamina-building for white educators. Without meeting these difficult dialogues head-on, young people continue to be negatively impacted by the lack of awareness and understanding held by adults.

Social Identity Profile

A number of exercises exist that allow individuals to reflect on our personal social identities—both ascribed (those that society thrusts upon us or that we are born into) as well as our self-claimed identities (those that might not be as clear). The identities educators hold impact the students, staff, and families they interact with. Actively engaging with the following questions becomes a critical part of being a culturally responsive educator:

- How does my understanding, or lack of understanding, of my own personal social identities impact how I navigate the world?
- How does my understanding, or lack of understanding, impact how I interact with my students, particularly those who hold differences in social identities?

The better we understand our own identities, the less likely we are to harm others and the more likely we are to build deeper relationships. About two decades ago, the University of Michigan's Center for Intergroup Relations developed the *Social Identity Profile*, and along with slight adaptations to the original exercise, it continues to hold tremendous potential in moving the work of CR-SE forward. The profile allows educators to take on an intersectional, reflective lens, in an effort to better understand self and personal impact on their surrounding community. The *Social Identity Profile* offers reflective prompts as individuals move through each of their social identities. Prompts include:

- Name the identity that gives me power and privilege in society . . .
- Name the identity I am most aware of . . .
- Name the identity that makes me uncomfortable to talk with others about . . .

From individuals with identities that hold power and privilege in U.S. society (e.g., white, cisgendered, nondisabled, English-speaking, heterosexual), we often hear reflections like "I have never thought about this before," highlighting the very need to critically self-reflect and move outside our default positions that often maintain systems of oppression. For individuals with identities that are targeted and marginalized in our society (e.g., Black, queer, disabled), it offers a space for validation, naming, and a further intersectional reflection across multiple identity markers.

DIRECTIONS FOR COMPLETING THE *SOCIAL IDENTITY PROFILE* YOURSELF AND/OR WITH A GROUP:

- To reiterate, the purpose of this tool is to build social identity self-reflection, to recognize intersecting forces of power and privilege, and to further understand the pervasive impact of racism from an intersectional lens (i.e., we hold all our identities as important to understand and how they change with context, while also holding the foundational impact of race and racism in the United States).
- Before jumping into this self-reflective work and sharing, individuals must agree on community norms to foster a brave space for those who hold power and privilege and a safe space for those who are historically and currently marginalized and can experience harm in dialogues across difference (see *"Setting the Table"* in Chapter 1). Be cognizant of the groupings, particularly thinking about individuals that may microaggress or invalidate another individual's experience.
- Make sure everyone has access to the *Social Identity Profile* handout (Chapter 2 appendices, Appendix E, https://www .tcpress.com/filebin/PDFs/9780807769447_app.pdf).

Process

1. Fill out the profile using the one side of the tool for reference (10–20 minutes). Make sure everyone knows the handout will not be collected and that they will end up sharing what they choose to share.
2. Do your best to write down your group membership for each row in the second column (using page 1 of the handout for support if needed).
3. This is not an exhaustive list—identities change and should be malleable. You should write in other identities in the "additional" space provided as needed (e.g., "mother." "immigrant" as additional).
4. In columns 3–11, mark only one identity that responds to the sentence stem in the header row. For example, only check "race" and not any other identities if that is what you are "most aware of" in column 3.
5. Remember to fill out the bottom blanks at the end of the profile.

Sharing Process

- As a facilitator, decide which questions you want the group to directly respond to after it is all filled out. Recommended: *"I think least about . . ."* *"Gives me power and privilege in society . . ."*
- Pair people together (2–3 in each group)
- Ask groups to individually share what they identified—each person has 60 seconds to respond/talk about it with their partner/group. For example, *"What did you identify for 'you think least about?'"*
- If they use 60 seconds, great; if not, hold air time and push participants to think about silent reflection and not filling space. This becomes an active listening practice as well.
- After a few rounds of questions (move from one sentence stem to the next, giving all individuals in the group time to respond), open to whole-group dialogue, highlighting the bottom question (*What two identities have the largest impact on your experience in your school/district?*).
- As the whole group shares takeaways from the process, ask individuals what patterns they are noticing. What identities are present in the group that provide power and privilege in society? Why is it important to be aware of both the identities in the room that are marginalized by society and those that give individuals power and privilege?

As evident in the directions above, there can be many layers to how this learning process is engaged. First and foremost, just the process of individually reflecting and filling out the handout provides another opportunity for embedded identity reflection—a muscle that we need to continuously grow as educators. The second layer to this process becomes the sharing. We appreciate what a timed sharing protocol can do to model how educators can develop comfort in what inevitably can be uncomfortable. The timed, 60-second sharing pushes individuals to jump in and helps curate a space where everyone has a voice. This can feel awkward for those who are already outspoken, and even more so for those who have relied on being silent. It also gives educators a sense of what is often asked of our students. In closing the learning process, it is important to reinforce how identity reflection is about developing an intersectional lens, where we are able to see how individuals can hold multiple marginalizations (e.g., Black, queer, English language learner). It is also critical to name where power and privilege lives within the social identities discussed. We often see white participants lean on talking about gender because they have more comfort in that dialogue as opposed to stepping into difficult conversations around race—being transparent about this as a facilitator is important in order to get the most out of this learning process.

CONNECTING SELF TO SYSTEM

As educators move through both the theoretical understanding of CR-SE while also engaging in the self-reflective work necessary to position one's own impact and experience with race, racism, power, privilege, and intersecting systems of oppression, it is critical that we continue to connect self-work to the systems work. Critical self-reflection cannot be the end all, be all—it must inform active and ongoing changes in practice, procedures, and policy implementation. For example, districts need to continually revise and create curricula that are culturally responsive. That said, this work will continue to be surface-level if individuals and systems are not simultaneously fostering a deeper, ongoing self-awareness. For example, a white cisgendered male history teacher must recognize how their identities impact the curriculum they deliver and the manner in which it is delivered. Whose voice are students hearing in this class? Has the teacher made space for counternarratives—centering nonwhite voices? And how is this more responsive practice outlined in the curriculum and across the history department to ensure every child is developing a critical consciousness, stretching well beyond white normative school culture? In an effort to continue to make self-to-system connections with real school-based realities, we have further provided several scenarios in the Chapter 2 appendices, Appendix F (https://www.tcpress.com/filebin/PDFs/9780807769447_app.pdf), for readers to move through individually and with colleagues.

In the next chapter we offer an in-depth look at our root cause analysis process. Analyzing student outcome and experience data as a part of a root cause analysis is a critical step in fostering culturally responsive communities. After moving through the learning processes in this chapter—centering the foundations of CR-SE and individual and institution critical self-reflective practice (Khalifa, 2018)—your district is primed for an effective root cause analysis and the action planning that follows.

CRITICAL QUESTIONS

1) Now, with a better understanding of CR-SE theory and practice, how are you thinking about your current role and the impact you are having on students, families, and colleagues?
2) How can you use the tools and learning processes outlined above to keep moving your district, and yourself, along your equity journey?
3) What are the immediate next steps you can take (e.g., filling out the *Social Identity Profile* with a colleague and talking about it)? What are the long-term next steps you can take to move you and your community forward (e.g., establishing school-based equity teams that move through creating a contract, using the language around equity tensions, and naming elephants in the room as a foundation to creating more culturally responsive classrooms and schools)?

CHAPTER 3

Understanding the Root Cause Analysis Process

CHAPTER OBJECTIVE:

The purpose of this chapter is to outline the processes and application tools districts can take to effectively address their disproportionality. We explain each phase of the process to help you more deeply understand the *why* and *how* of the work, including centering CR-SE and the work of critical self-reflection and interrogating the impact of social identities.

Elmer City School District has continuously struggled with over-classifying Black students into special education, and once Black students are classified with an IEP, they experience higher suspension rates. To that end, Elmer received a notification for 4a/4b (see the Glossary) for multiple years (2012–2013 to 2015–2016) and significant disproportionality (school year 2012–2013) from the state's Office of Special Education for exceeding the state threshold (see Table 3.1 for state threshold and Table 3.2 for citation data). From 2012–2013 to 2014–2015, Elmer exceeded the threshold for Black and Latinx students, and then again for only Black students in 2015–2016.

More often than not, for Elmer and other districts, disproportionality that exists in suspending children with an IEP also mirrors suspension patterns for non-IEP students (Hernández et al., 2023). Elmer was also a district that was investigated by the state attorney general for their disciplinary practices that led to in-school suspensions (ISSs) or out-of-school suspensions (OOSs) for Black children. The attorney general highlighted in their report that Elmer's suspension rate was one of the highest in the nation.

Elmer is not unique to racial disproportionality that lives in schools. Education disproportionality is a chronic issue that continues to impact

Table 3.1. State Citation Thresholds by Year for 4a/4b and Significant Disproportionality

Year	2012–13	2013–14	2014–15	2015–16	2016–17	2017–18	2018–19
Citation Criteria Indicator 4a: Number of school-going children with disabilities suspended over 10 days	2.70%	2.70%	2.70%	2.70%	2.70%	2.70%	2.70%
Citation Criteria Indicator 4b: Number of school-going children with disabilities suspended over 10 days by race	3.49%	3.21%	3.07%	2.98%	3.03%	3.03%	3.08%
Significant disproportionality	2.0	2.0	2.0	2.0	2.0	2.0	2.0

the experiences and outcomes of students of color (in particular Black, Latinx, and Indigenous/Native), students with an IEP, and multilingual learners and students holding these intersecting identities (Hernández et al., 2023). While many have identified solutions to tackle disproportionality (Kozleski & Artiles, 2012), the applicable tools and processes that support districts and schools in addressing their disproportionality remain limited, with the exception of Fergus (2017) and Fergus and Ahram (2009).

A root cause analysis offers districts and schools a comprehensive process to critically engage qualitative and quantitative data; examine the beliefs, policies, procedures, and practices that are leading to inequities; and target action steps that can remedy disparate experiences and outcomes for the students and families most impacted. Further, a root cause analysis approach aims to collaborate with, listen to, and build relationships with and in communities that question disproportionality to ultimately disrupt educational inequities (San Pedro & Kinloch, 2017). An effective root cause analysis seeks to unearth the inequities that exist in a given community, to give voice to those historically and currently marginalized, and to support the development of protective spaces for

Table 3.2. Elmer Citation Data Patterns 2012–13 to 2018–2019: Significant Discrepancy and Disproportionality

Notification Year	Indicator 4a (Significant Discrepancy) Suspension Rate	Indicator 4b (Significant Discrepancy) Suspension Rate	Significant Disproportionality Relative Risk (OSS>10)
2012–13	All SWDs*— 5.50%***	Black SWDs—6.79%***	Black SWDs 2.55
		White SWDs—3.64%	
		Latinx SWDs—5.35%***	
2013–14	All SWDs— 4.70%***	Black SWDs—6.13%***	Not Cited
		White SWDs—2.89% (At-Risk)	
		Latinx SWDs—3.85%***	
2014–15	All SWDs— 4.40%***	Black SWDs—5.65%***	Not Cited
		White SWDs—2.88% (At-Risk)	
		Latinx SWDs—3.66%***	
2015–16	All SWDs— 2.50% (At-Risk)	Black SWDs—3.17%***	Not Cited
		White SWDs—1.53% (At-Risk)	
		Latinx SWDs—2.32% (At-Risk)	
2016–17	Not Cited	Not Cited	Not Cited
2017–18	Not Cited	Not Cited	Not Cited
2018-19**	Not Cited	Not Cited	Not Cited

*SWD: Students with disabilities
**Limited access to state citation data
***Exceeds state threshold

vulnerable communities, which inevitably strengthens the community at large. In our work with districts, just targeting a singular policy or practice or looking at select data will fail to fully unveil the processes leading to disproportionality. A robust and strategic audit is necessary to adequately inform a multiyear action plan that will lead to systemic change (Valdez et al., 2020). Elmer's initial journey started with our root cause analysis process that led to unveiling the beliefs, policies, practices, and procedures that led to their race-based disproportionality.

Chapter 4 will offer a more hands-on example of each phase to directly support walking you and your team through all of the steps described in this chapter. Further, in Chapter 4 we will use an example district for you to practice analyzing with your team to then effectively move to looking at your own district data policies, procedures, and practices. We see Chapters 3 and 4 as an *I Do, We Do, You Do* gradual release approach!

Table 3.3 lays out some of the key root cause analysis processes we want you to understand before applying it in Chapter 4.

FRAMING THE IMPORTANCE OF THE ROOT CAUSE PROCESS

The purpose of a root cause analysis process is for a district to identify the beliefs, policies, procedures, and practices that are leading to disparate experiences and outcomes for historically and currently marginalized students (Hernández et al., 2023). We offer a capacity-building approach by employing an evidence-based root cause analysis process that examines both quantitative and qualitative data and beliefs, policies, practices, and procedures to unveil root causes of disproportionality (see Figure 3.1). The process builds understanding of the causes of disproportionality and the compounding factors that lead to inequalities in order to fully unveil root causes and effectively engage action planning. The goals of the root cause analysis are to (a) identify the possible root causes and compounding factors of disproportionality; (b) examine and identify beliefs, policies, and practices that contribute to disparate outcomes; (c) explore how race, culture, power, and privilege perpetuate disproportionality; and (d) develop a plan designed to address identified causes (see Figure 3.1 for the root cause sequence).

PRECONDITIONS FOR ROOT CAUSE ANALYSIS

A central prerequisite for districts and schools aiming to address their race-based disproportionality is that they must be open to grappling with addressing who is most impacted in their school community (Bryk et al., 2015; Valdez et al., 2020). As such, one of the remedies to address disproportionality is to acknowledge the impact of race and racism on children of color and families (Carter et al., 2017). Without centering the students and families impacted by inequities, systems continue to maintain the same experience of harm and outcomes for students and families of color (in particular Black, Latinx, and Indigenous/Native), children with an IEP, and multilingual learners (Milner et al., 2020).

Table 3.3. Key Understanding of Root Cause Process

Root Cause Steps to Deeper Understanding	Key Questions	Example and Tools
Readiness Tool	*Are we ready to address our disproportionality? What did the readiness tool findings highlight for your district?*	Complete District Task: Assessing Readiness and Chapter 3, Appendix A*
Moral Imperative	*Why is this work important and how will you communicate it?*	See Chapter 4 for an example to develop your own moral imperative. (Explanation below.)
Behavior and Academic Workbook Data Analysis	*What data systems do you currently use? Will it allow you to disaggregate data by race/ethnicity, gender, and students with an IEP? Who in your district can do this?*	Tables 3.4 and 3.5 and Chapter 3, Appendices E and F*
Methods of Calculating Disproportionality	*Do you understand how you will calculate your disproportionality?*	
Foundational Readings	*What connections are you making between your district and readings?*	Complete Chapter 3, Appendices C and D*
Parent/Caregiver and Student Focus Groups	*What information would you want to hear from historically and currently marginalized students and parents/caregivers about their experiences in the district?* *Have you identified an outside consultant who is trained in qualitative methods and interviewing to conduct the **focus group** and/or **listening sessions** and complete the analysis?*	Chapter 3, Appendices G and H*
Code of Conduct	*How do individual schools apply the code of conduct?* *What current information do you currently have that offers insight into how individual schools implement the code of conduct?*	Chapter 3, Appendix I*

(continued)

Table 3.3. (continued)

Root Cause Steps to Deeper Understanding	Key Questions	Example and Tools
Discipline Referral Form	*Does the discipline referral form operate as a tool for learning and support for educators and students? How is the discipline referral form used?*	Chapter 3, Appendix J*
Intervention Inventory	*How are tiered academic and behavioral interventions grounded in cultural responsiveness?*	Chapter 3, Appendix K
Root Cause Hypothesis	*How will you center your hypothesis to drive your next steps and avoid detours?*	See Chapter 4, Table 4.37 Root Cause Hypothesis. (Explanation below.)

*https://www.tcpress.com/filebin/PDFs/9780807769447_app.pdf

Within their framework for *levels of resistance and engagement,* Hernández and colleagues (2023) lay out the conditions that districts and schools will have to grapple with to tackle their disproportionality. This includes (a) having an overall understanding of why a district/school desires to address their disproportionality; (b) considering a moral imperative for the work; (c) coordinating the logistics for the work; (d) getting critical buy-in specifically from district leadership; (e) dissemination and follow-up, including communicating the work that is occurring; and (f) carrying out an assessment of the beliefs and attitudes that exist in the district community (e.g., denying that disproportionality exists in their district and schools, dismissing/minimizing race and racism; see Chapter 1). Hernández et al. (2023) underscore that districts and schools must be informed of the levels of resistance and engagement as part of the challenges that they may experience as they become potential barriers to forward movement. Not acknowledging them, nor directly addressing them, will maintain schooling experiences that continue to replicate the same experiences and outcomes for historically and currently marginalized students (Carter et al., 2017).

Additionally, the preconditions necessary to engage the root cause process underscore that districts and schools must engage a collaborative approach, understanding that building an ongoing inquiry focus is the most impactful approach to systemic change (Kozleski & Artiles,

Figure 3.1. Root Cause: Importance of the Work

We conduct a six-part equity audit series that identifies root causes of inequitable outcomes. The goal of the root cause analysis is to: (1) identify the possible root causes and compounding factors of disproportionality and larger inequities, (2) examine and identify beliefs, policies, practices, and procedures that contribute to disparate outcomes, (3) explore how race, culture, power and privilege perpetuate inequities and disproportionality, (4) develop a coherent research based plan designed to address identified root causes. IESC will achieve these goals through an iterative process of facilitated meetings, TA, data collection, and analysis.

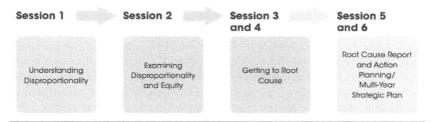

2012). To that end, districts and schools must bring together diverse stakeholders that include parents/caregivers, local teachers, paraprofessionals, pupil support staff, district and school leaders, and board members who hold different roles and social identity markers (race, gender, sexuality, among others). This team can offer insight into the experiences that students and families are having that offers a local, contextualized examination of the beliefs, policies, procedures, and practices leading to their disproportionality.

Readiness to Address Disproportionality: A District Readiness Tool

Research has underscored that there are some foundational readiness elements needed for organizational change. Organizations must develop a cohesive group with shared values, a collective vision, and clear expectations of what they are hoping to accomplish (Rushovich et al., 2015). Readiness for change and buy-in from leadership is critical for work to move forward and for project implementation (Bryk et al., 2010). When buy-in is absent or weak, it is a major barrier to successful implementation (Rushovich et al., 2015). That is, when districts/organizations—and the individuals within them—are not primed for the work, systems change becomes increasingly difficult. In districts, in order to message the work, leaders must have a clear moral imperative and vision of why they want to tackle their disproportionality, a longstanding commitment to the work, and an understanding that it will not be a quick fix (Fullan & Quinn, 2016; Hernández et al., 2023).

Our readiness tool, which assesses a district's readiness to address disproportionality, centers on three focal areas: (a) the school district recognizing that race-based disproportionality exists in the district and schools; (b) the infrastructure (e.g., instruction support systems, academic support systems) that exists in the district to address disproportionality, including systems that are implemented with commitment; and (c) school and district leaders' capacity to build systems within each domain supports (professional staff capacity, instructional guidance, student-centered learning climate, and family/community partnerships; Bryk et al., 2010) to address disparate outcomes (see Chapter 3 appendices, Appendix A, https://www.tcpress.com/filebin/PDFs/9780807769447_app.pdf). The readiness tool, highlighting these three domains, offers a gauge of a district's readiness to address their disproportionality. A 0–4 Likert scale ranging from "never" to "all the time" is used and a composite score is calculated to assess readiness. The scores align with a level of readiness criteria. For example, the readiness criterion ranges from *No Awareness* to *Awareness* (see Chapter 3 appendices, Appendix A, https://www.tcpress.com/filebin/PDFs/9780807769447_app.pdf). Descriptors for districts who fall in *No Awareness* include the district denying that they have a problem with disproportionality and perceiving inappropriate classifications and suspensions for certain student groups as part of common practices. The result is a snapshot of the district's readiness to begin addressing issues related to disproportionality, and highlights that tackling their disproportionality would not be a quick fix.

DISTRICT TASK: ASSESSING READINESS

This task offers an opportunity for you and a root cause team to engage in assessing your readiness. Before starting the root cause analysis process, the root cause team should complete the readiness tool worksheet. Alternatively, when a district is uncertain if they are ready to start tackling their disproportionality, a curated team with different roles and social identities should complete the readiness tool worksheet. Regardless of whether it is a root cause team or a curated team who wants to explore their district's readiness, each team separately completes the readiness tool worksheet and shares their results with other team members. A team member then charts the findings for all teams, and the teams then have a discussion on their agreements and discrepancies in scoring and in what continuum of readiness they fall into, *No Awareness* to *Awareness*. This process offers a starting point for where the district is and gives insight into what needs to be kept in mind moving forward.

Readiness to Address Disproportionality:
Moral Imperative Development

One of the critical phases of the root cause analysis process is to develop a moral imperative that serves to lift the importance of the work and to support the message of the work to multiple stakeholders. A moral imperative connects individuals to their moral purpose to education and builds a deeper understanding of stakeholders' collective moral imperative (Fullan & Quinn, 2016). Chapter 4 walks your district team through the steps of creating a collective moral imperative and offers an example.

THE ROOT CAUSE ANALYSIS PROCESS

Once a district assesses their readiness for the work and develops a moral imperative statement, the first phase of a root cause analysis includes setting the norms and expectations (see Chapter 1 for a description of how to set up *norms*) of how the root cause team will engage together and up front, noting the core tensions that arise when working to achieve racial equity (Pollock et al., 2010). Another critical aspect of creating norms and expectations for root cause team members is to identify the students and families most disproportionately impacted in your specific district and school community (see "Naming the Elephants in the Room" in Chapter 1). To that end, it is critical that the root cause community develops the skill to identify who is impacted by disproportionality and move through the tensions (Pollock et al., 2010). Moreover, when the communities most impacted are not discussed, are "othered" and not named, a district and school will be unable to address the disproportionate experiences and outcomes that exist (Carter et al., 2017; Hernández et al., 2023). Another caution when *naming the elephants in the room* is that nonwhite students with differences in ability—Black, Latinx, and Indigenous/Native children in particular—and students who are poor are often othered. The language used may include "those kids," "these kids," or "those who live *over there*." It is important that the team ask clarifying questions such as, Which children are you referring to from our "elephants in the room?" Can you be specific as to which community of students you are talking about?

Once norms and expectations of what will occur in the root cause process have been established, additional aims of the root cause process include developing a common understanding of disproportionality, how it relates to a district's data, and how to build the capacity of both the individual participants and the district to effectively address disproportionality. Another process the root cause team will engage in is unpacking data workbooks (see examples in Table 3.4 and Table 3.5) compiled for the district and school-level teams and offer them as examples to demonstrate what disaggregated data should look like.

The district-level data book provides practitioners with the opportunity to explore district-level data to further understand disciplinary and academic outcome patterns across the district as a whole. The root cause team collectively will review school district data, coupled with policies, procedures, and practices, to identify and map the causes of disproportionality (see Chapter 4 for guided application examples). Districts analyze student-level academic and discipline outcome data disaggregated by race/ethnicity, sex, grade, and IEP status. In this analysis for discipline, the following are included: (a) the district enrollment, (b) the number of behavioral incidents, (c) the number of students involved in the behavioral incidents, and (d) the number of discipline referrals, IEP classifications/declassifications, and suspensions. The academic analysis includes (a) the district enrollment, (b) ELA/Math benchmark data, (c) the rate that students are passing or failing courses they are enrolled in, and (d) the number of students enrollment in gifted/talented programs, AP/Honor/IB (International Baccalaureate) enrollment, and extracurricular activities. For each of these workbooks, the composition index, risk ratio, and the relative risk ratio are calculated (see the description below). This data analysis is used to further understand what students are most disproportionately impacted in general education and by special education assignment and within the discipline system (through behavioral referrals and suspensions) and academic systems (see Chapter 3 appendices, Appendix B, for guiding questions; https://www.tcpress.com/filebin/PDFs/9780807769447_app.pdf). The following section offers specifics on the behavioral and academic workbooks.

ROOT CAUSE ANALYSIS TOOLS

Foundational Readings

Part of the root causes analysis process is for the root cause team to also ground themselves in critical readings to build their collective understanding of the work. As preparation to engage the root causes process in Chapter 4, your root cause team should move forward with foundational readings. In our work, we have experienced critical breakthroughs resulting from the dialogues that occur in response to the readings.

Table 3.4. 2018–2019 District Suspension Relative Risk by Race/Ethnicity, Gender, and IEP Status

2018–19	Suspension Relative Risks					
	Indigenous/ Native	Asian or Pacific Islander	Black or African American	Latinx	White (not of Latino/a Origin)	Multiracial
Relative Risk of Suspensions	3.74	0.98	2.98	1.48	0.3	2.42
Relative Risk of Students Suspended	2.44	1.13	3.68	1.11	0.45	2.20
Gender						
Relative Risk of Female Suspensions	5.22	1.08	4.82	1.76	0.24	2.29
Relative Risk of Female Students Suspended	3.38	1.69	7.49	0.72	0.41	2.48
Relative Risk of Male Suspensions	2.99	1.29	2.17	1.40	0.34	2.31
Relative Risk of Male Students Suspended	1.95	0.99	2.22	1.36	0.47	1.96
IEP						
Relative Risk of IEP Suspensions	2.08	3.50	1.29	3.37	0.26	1.33
Relative Risk of IEP Students Suspended	1.61	2.80	2.09	1.50	0.46	1.75
Relative Risk of Non-IEP Suspensions	4.48	0.63	3.89	0.95	0.34	2.94
Relative Risk of Non-IEP Students Suspended	2.69	0.95	4.39	1.01	0.46	2.32

Table 3.5. District 2018–2019 and 2019–2022 AP Enrollment by Race/Ethnicity

		AP Enrollment					
2018–19	Indigenous/ Native	Asian or Pacific Islander	Black or African American	Latinx	White (not of Latino/a Origin)	Multiracial
Composition of Students Enrolled	5.0%	2.20%	0.90%	13.40%	67.80%	9.50%
Composition AP Enrollment by Race	1.90%	3.40%	0.60%	10.20%	75.80%	7.50%
Risk Index AP Enrollment by Race	7.20%	30.60%	13.30%	14.90%	21.90%	15.30%
2019–20						
Composition of Students Enrolled	4.80%	2.10%	1.0%	14.20%	67.0%	9.4%
Composition AP Enrollment by Race	1.40%	4.40%	0.70%	10.50%	72.60%	9.10%
Risk Index AP Enrollment by Race	4.80%	36.10%	11.80%	12.70%	18.70%	16.70%

DISTRICT TASK: FOUNDATIONAL READINGS

Moving through the foundational readings becomes a collective inquiry process that supports teams. It will take 1–1.5 hours to unpack each reading set (see Chapter 3 appendices, Appendix C for a reading list; https://www.tcpress.com/filebin/PDFs/9780807769447_app.pdf). The root cause community can take sections of the reading and unpack them in groups of 4–5 depending on the size of the team. The team should have some guiding questions for the readings (see Chapter 3 appendices, Appendix D for a reading worksheet; https://www.tcpress .com/filebin/PDFs/9780807769447_app.pdf).

Outcome Data Collection and Analysis: Behavior and Academic Workbooks

The behavior and academic workbooks offer educators a tool to examine who is most disproportionately impacted in a school setting. This tool calculates different common disproportionality calculation methods alongside disaggregation of data by race/ethnicity, sex, students with an IEP/non-IEP, and the intersectionality of identities. The district workbook offers a bird's-eye view of analysis by examining overall patterns that exist in the district. The school-level workbooks offer a more micro-level examination of student outcomes in schools. It is important to conduct both data analysis of district- and school-level data to identify the student communities having disparate experiences and outcomes. It is also important to hold that disproportionality is not simply a school issue; rather, it is the result of a district's system, including beliefs, policies, procedures, and practices (Fergus, 2017; Hernández et al., 2023; Klingner et al., 2005).

Discipline Workbook. The discipline workbook data (see Chapter 3 appendices, Appendix E, https://www.tcpress.com/filebin/PDFs/97808077 69447_app.pdf) is tabulated in two different ways: by student and by discipline referral. Student data counts each student for whom there is a discipline record regardless of how many times the student has been referred for disciplinary action. Referral data count the total number of discipline referrals, but do not take into account that certain students are counted multiple times. That is:

- Count of Students: Count of each student for whom there is a discipline record regardless of how many times the student has been referred for disciplinary action. A student is counted only once.

- X Count of Referrals: Count of total number of infractions; students can be counted multiple times.

Academic Workbook. Academic data are one of the key indicators to assess districts' and schools' success with students. The academic workbooks offer various academic data points to examine student academic outcome patterns (see Chapter 3 appendices, Appendix F, https://www.tcpress.com/filebin/PDFs/9780807769447_app.pdf). The focus on using varied academic data points (such as ELA/math benchmark data and student course passing and failure rates usage) instead of state testing is to develop a more nuanced view and accurate assessment of the academic trajectories of different students (e.g., Black males, Black females with an IEP). This data examination provides a closer look to help identify the intervention supports and access to programming and services that aim to improve student outcomes. This initial look at your district's data is meant to provide a framework to both examine disproportionate student performance and achievement outcomes, and help your team pose focused questions on the root causes that lead to disparate academic outcomes and, most importantly, to take action. Similar to the behavior workbook, the academic workbook highlights (a) the demographics of students enrolled in the district; (b) the assessments used; (c) the outcomes of the assessment and the level of student proficiency on the assessments; (d) the examination of the scores by race, sex, students with an IEP, and intersectionality across multiple identity markers.

Methods for Calculating Disproportionality

The data analysis process uses three prominent methods to calculate disproportionality: composition index, risk index, and relative risk ratio. You can use the guide below to further develop your community's ability to calculate your disproportionality. Pushback and defensiveness around data become commonplace as individuals and communities resist equity work. For this reason, it is important that local communities develop the capacity to calculate and more deeply understand their disproportionality.

Composition Index Calculation. The composition index gives the proportion of students by race/ethnicity in a particular outcome. Composition indexes are used to determine if a particular group is over- or underrepresented in a particular outcome. Table 3.6 provides the mathematical calculation of the composition index.

In Table 3.6, the *Number of Students in an Outcome* row focuses on a specific outcome (e.g., the number of students referred for discipline) by race/ethnicity. To calculate the composition of a student group in an outcome, the number of students in an outcome is divided by the total

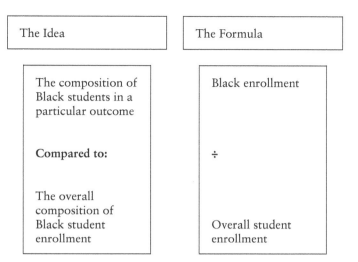

The Idea	The Formula
The composition of Black students in a particular outcome	Black enrollment
Compared to:	÷
The overall composition of Black student enrollment	Overall student enrollment

Table 3.6. Calculating the Composition Index

	Indigenous/ Native	Asian	Black	Latinx	White	Multiracial	Total
Number of Students in an Outcome	A	B	C	D	E	F	A+B+ C+D+ E+F=G
Overall Student Enrollment	H	I	J	K	L	M	H+I+J+ K+L+ M=N
Composition of a Student Group in an Outcome	A/G	B/G	C/G	D/G	E/G	F/G	100%
Composition of Student Enrollment	H/N	I/N	J/N	K/N	L/N	M/N	100%

number of students in the outcome. That is, for Latinx students, dividing D by G would calculate the percentage of Latinx students who are experiencing that specific outcome. Similarly, to calculate student enrollment for Latinx students, D is divided by N. By calculating both the composition of student enrollment and the composition of a student group in an outcome, the disproportionate over- or underrepresentation of a student group can be determined. For example, that would read as Latinx students make up 25% of a school population but receive 50% of all suspensions in a given year. This would signify that Latinx students are overrepresented in suspensions.

Risk Index/Rate Calculation. Risk Index/Rate is the representation of a racial/ethnic group in a particular outcome in comparison to the total enrollment of that specific racial/ethnic group.

The Idea	The Formula
The risk of Black students being suspended	Black students suspended
Compared to	÷
Rate of Black student enrollment	Black enrollment

For example, 30 Black students are involved in the disciplinary outcome out of a total 100 Black students enrolled. The Risk Index or Rate for Black students stands at 30%. In other words, Black students are at a 30% risk of being represented in a disciplinary action.

Relative Risk Ratio Calculation. Relative Risk Ratio, also referred to as "relative risk," is the risk of one racial/ethnic group in comparison to the risk of all other racial/ethnic groups to experience an outcome. A risk ratio of 1 indicates a racial/ethnic group has equal risk in comparison to all other groups for a particular outcome; less than 1 means underrepresentation of a racial/ethnic group; higher than 1 means that a racial/ethnic group is at an elevated risk in comparison to the other racial/ethnic groups.

For example, if 50 out of 100 Black students were suspended, that's a risk of 50%, whereas if only 50 out of 200 students from all other racial/ethnic groups were suspended, that's a risk of 25%. Fifty percent is divided by 25%, and the relative risk ratio for Black students is 2, which means Black students are 2 times more likely to be suspended as compared to all other students. The relative risk ratio is often a preferred method of calculation, as it offers a comparative index of risk (Klingner et al., 2005).

| The Idea | The Formula |

The Risk of Black Students Being Suspended	(Black students suspended ÷ Black enrollment)
Compared to	÷
The Risk of All Other Students Being Suspended (Not Including Black Students)	[(Total suspensions − Black suspension) ÷ (Total enrollment − Black enrollment)]

Parent/Caregiver and Student Focus Groups

Bryk et al. (2015) underscore that it is critical that districts and schools consult the people on the ground who know most about the problem and who are most impacted by it. To that end, districts and schools must speak to the parents/caregivers and students who are most impacted by disproportionality. Through focus group interviews, district and school personnel gather insight into the experiences students and parents/caregivers are having in schooling spaces. By hearing from the communities directly impacted instead of those who have always benefited from the educational process, these data will offer a counternarrative, which is often a paradigm shift from the ways in which districts have continued to operate and maintain systemic inequities (Milner et al., 2020). Such an approach underscores the significance of centering students and families most disproportionately impacted and challenging those who only hold quantitative data as truth.

The parent/caregiver and student focus group protocols in Chapter 3, Appendices G and H (https://www.tcpress.com/filebin/PDFs/97808077 69447_app.pdf), ask participants grounding questions that center their experiences in the respective district and schools, including overall likes and dislikes, race-based experiences, and what the district and their school could do better. Further, the parent/caregiver interview protocol underscores how the school their child attends engages them as a parent/caregiver and values their input, and how much the school leader engages them in decision-making processes. The student interviews aim to capture school culture, student and adult interactions, and students' views on who makes them feel successful in school. It is important to contract an outside consultant who is trained in qualitative methods and interviewing when conducting **focus group** and/or **listening sessions**.

Policy Analysis: Code of Conduct

District and school policies guide the daily procedures and operations of districts and schools. In a root cause analysis process, the analysis of central policies offer insight into how policies are impacting a district and school communities. One of the policies that districts must review is the code of conduct. Often the purpose and language in the code of conduct are correlated to the practices enacted in schools, ultimately leading to referrals and suspensions. To that end, a critical part of the root cause process is to unveil how the code of conduct as a policy leads to referrals and suspensions. In this review of the code of conduct, the perspective of the district root cause team is central. They are best equipped to offer the context to the code of conduct, including the purpose, development, and implementation. Once the team completes the code of conduct review, they then identify the strengths, weaknesses, and gaps in the document to pinpoint actionable steps. Review the code of conduct questions in the Chapter 3 appendices, Appendix I (https://www.tcpress.com/filebin/PDFs/9780807769447_app .pdf), before moving on to Chapter 4.

Discipline Referral Form. The discipline referral form documents referral incidents and the outcomes related to discipline referrals. The root cause team also completes an analysis of the discipline referral forms. The district should gather all the formal and informal discipline referral forms that schools use. Members of the root cause team who are district leaders are paramount in reviewing the discipline referral form, as they are best equipped to offer the context of the purpose and usage of the form itself. It is important to keep in mind that the analysis may not reflect all of the processes/procedures that the district/schools follow. To that end, it is essential to also hear from voices who are not in the root cause process to gather further information about additional processes/ procedures that are being followed. Once the team completes the discipline referral form review, they identify the strengths, weaknesses, and gaps of the discipline referral to pinpoint actionable steps. Review the discipline referral questions in the Chapter 3 appendices, Appendix J (https://www.tcpress.com/filebin/PDFs/9780807769447_app.pdf), before moving on to Chapter 4.

Analyzing Practices: Intervention Inventory

The purpose of analysis of the multitiered interventions and supports is to assess the level of tiered support, identify how students are referred, and identify how the progress and implementation of interventions are monitored. For instance, Tier 1 academics are universally aiming to reach the majority of students and include high-quality, research-based, differentiated instruction; collaborative teaming in general and special education; and data-driven decisions (McIntosh & Goodman, 2016). Ideally, Tier 2 offers targeted intervention support that addresses students' specific skill needs without replacing high-quality, research-based, differentiated instruction and data-driven decision-making. Tier 3 should increase the intensity of students' targeted intervention, including individualized intervention support, and does not replace high-quality, research-based, differentiated instruction and data-driven decision-making (McIntosh & Goodman, 2016). See the Massachusetts Department of Elementary and Secondary Education (MDESE) blueprint at https://www.doe.mass.edu/sfss/mtss/blueprint.pdf for further information. The purpose of the intervention inventory is for districts and schools to assess their tiered academic and behavior interventions and identify what is available for students and what intervention gaps may exist (see Chapter 3 appendices, Appendix K, https://www.tcpress.com/filebin/PDFs/9780807769447_app.pdf).

During the root cause process, the curated root cause team completes the intervention inventory with educators from elementary, middle, and high school levels. The team offers a comprehensive list of academic and behavior interventions, including their purpose, how interventions are evaluated for implementation fidelity, and how progress is monitored. They are also assessing how data are used and, foundationally, determining if the interventions are culturally responsive for students. Once the team completes the intervention inventory, the next step is to synthesize the information from the Chapter 3 appendices, Appendix K (https://www.tcpress.com/filebin/PDFs/9780807769447_app.pdf), and use the Intervention Inventory in Appendix K to move on to the next steps. These next steps should include (1) identifying the intervention gaps, (2) identifying goals to address the gaps and a clear timeline for completion, (3) deciding who will be responsible for task completion, and (4) deciding how often the team who is addressing the intervention gaps will meet to assess their progress.

Root Cause Hypothesis and Next Steps

Once the curated root cause team has examined the district- and school-level workbooks, reviewed the students and parent/caregiver focus group analysis, and completed the policy and practice analysis processes, they will solidify the root causes associated with their disproportionality to inform action steps. The hypothesis process informs the next actionable steps districts will take to tackle the identified areas of disproportionality (see Chapter 4). This includes developing a targeted multiyear plan that derives from the root causes. The plan should include S.M.A.R.T. goals,[1] strategies to implement S.M.A.R.T. goals, a timeline, and a process for deciding who is responsible for leading and supporting the implementation process (see Chapter 4).

PROMISING SYSTEM SHIFTS

We return to Elmer City School District to underscore the next steps that took place across the elementary, middle, and high schools following the root cause analysis. They identified the following next steps:

1) Training staff in culturally responsive education
2) Restorative practices training
3) Classroom management training
4) Creating access to more effective disciplinary models and acquiring more effective intervention programs for behavior
5) Hiring mediation specialists and coaches
6) Reviewing whole-school data and individual data, and putting interventions into place, along with monitoring progress
7) Sharing suspension and disproportionate data with all staff
8) Training on the student code of conduct
9) Training on how to engage parents/caregivers

Moreover, Elmer committed to the use of disaggregated data to inform decision-making. They adopted an equity-based solution process that uses disaggregated academic and behavior data to inform decision-making in schools to shift beliefs, policies, procedures, and practices (BPPPs) that were still leading to disparate outcomes. School-level teams that included the building principal or assistant principal attended the sessions to build specific school plans that focused on disproportionate data outcomes of the students who were primarily impacted. The schools that consistently attended the meetings shared in sessions that they started, and saw some shifts in their disciplinary referral and suspension data. Alongside the data work, schools were still developing structures and supports to respond to the behavioral needs by identifying alternate ways to support and redirect student behavior rather than resorting to referrals and suspensions, including restorative practice and Positive Behavior Interventions and Supports (PBIS) training. Immediately, with support from the Office Pupil Support Services, each school was asked to create a behavioral intervention classroom (BIC), where students could take time out to reflect. The goal was to have students process how they were feeling, share with an adult what was going on, and return to their classrooms. Overall, by monitoring disaggregated discipline data and identifying action steps, Elmer began to observe changes in their referral and suspension data (see Table 3.7 and Table 3.8).

Table 3.7. Changes in Behavioral Referrals by Race

	2014–15	2015–16	2016–17	2017–18	Overall Shift*
Black	21,885	20,498	11,927	13,003	−40.6%
Latinx	–	3,453	2,154	2,238	–
White	6,931	4,893	2,649	2,186	−68.5%
Asian	455	275	147	152	−66.6%
Indigenous	382	455	182	173	−54.7%
Multiracial	1,207	0	982	1,063	−11.9
All Students	30,860	29,574	18,041	18,815	−39.0%

*The decline total is based on subtracting the final year's referrals from the beginning year's referrals.

Table 3.8. Changes in Suspensions by Race

	2014–15	2015–16	2016–17	2017–18	Overall Shifts*
Black	8,670	7,111	5,867	5,911	−31.8%
Latinx	1,436	1,316	1,118	1,028	−28.4%
White	1,816	1,610	1,137	1,005	−44.7%
Asian	177	104	86	77	−56.5%
Indigenous	357	0	374	406	13.7%
Multiracial	126	150	82	108	−14.3%
All Students	12,582	10,291	8,664	8,535	−32.2%

*The decline total is based on subtracting the final year's suspensions from the beginning year's suspensions.

CONCLUSION

This chapter has offered a pathway for districts and schools to engage their disproportionality head-on. As highlighted in this chapter, focusing on the preconditions is the first step:

- Focusing on the children and families mostly impacted by disproportionality
- Selecting a team with different social identity markers and roles
- Developing and messaging the moral imperative for the work
- Completing filling out the readiness tool worksheet

The root cause process provides the path districts will embark on. This path includes:

- Engaging the root cause team in critical reflective readings
- Examining disaggregated academic and behavior data to identify which students are most impacted by disproportionality
- Hearing from students and families regarding their experiences through listening sessions
- Examining policies such as the code of conduct
- Analyzing practices such as the behavior referral form, as well as academic and behavior intervention and supports for students
- Postulating hypotheses to unveil the root causes of your district's disproportionality

Chapter 4 offers direct application of the root cause process through the use of a sample district. This scaffolded application will propel your district team to then use your own data to effectively carry out your district's root cause process.

Through dozens of partnering districts, like Elmer, we have seen shifts in beliefs, policies, and practices as a result of the methodical root cause approach highlighted in this chapter. Elmer is a critical example of what happens when a district makes a commitment to sustain a practice of making shifts in practices and procedures that are informed by data. Elmer generated steady shifts in their suspension disparities through a continued practice of analyzing data and examining their BPPPs connected to data, while also developing solutions to center students who were mostly impacted (e.g., Black students, Black students with an IEP). We encourage readers to take the time to think through each step, recognizing that this work takes time and commitment; however, once you start the journey of addressing your disproportionality, tangible shifts are possible.

CRITICAL QUESTIONS

1) Who is mostly impacted by disproportionality in your district?
2) What can be the first steps in your district to address your disproportionality?
3) Whose voices do you usually include on your teams? Whose voices are usually missing on your teams?

Applying an Inquiry Approach

An Example Root Cause Analysis Process

> What would our equity approach be if we met people who bear the
> weight of institutional racism or ableism where *they* are? What if we
> heeded their demand for something more meaningful than baby steps?
>
> —Gorski et al. (2022)

In Chapter 1, we explained what it means to "set the table" for successful district equity shifts—learning to *name the elephants in the room* and
move with *racial equity tensions.* These processes and commitments push
us to keep the voices and experiences of children and families most impacted at the center of the work (Bryk et al., 2015). Chapter 2 offered examples illustrating that without the adaptive, heart work, the technical side
of dismantling disproportionality will continue to fall short (Hernández
et al., 2023). In the previous chapter we walked through our root cause
analysis process to provide the "why" of undertaking an equity audit and
to offer an in-depth understanding of each phase in the process.

In this chapter we will move from describing the root cause analysis
process in Chapter 3 to practicing the process. What follows is a step-
by-step guide to move through with your district team. We lay out each
step of the root cause process as it was laid out in the previous chapter,
but here we provide Garner Central School District as an example (a very
real district we worked with—we are using a pseudonym for confidentiality purposes). While highlighting these in-district examples, we pose
questions as you analyze the data offered. This scaffolded approach will
ready your team to engage your own full root cause analysis and the
subsequent action planning that follows by using the templates offered
in the appendices.

Table 4.1 lists the root cause analysis phases you will move through.
Each phase has examples from Garner Central School District alongside instructions for you and your team to follow when you use your
own data.

Table 4.1. Root Cause Application Tasks

Root Cause Phase	Application Task
Developing a Moral Imperative	**Time:** Up to 3 hours **Groups:** ~ 5 individuals per team **Task:** Develop and share personal moral imperatives that ultimately lead to a finalized, group/district moral imperative statement.
Analyzing Academic Data	**Time:** Up to 3 hours for district- and school-level workbooks **Groups:** ~ 4–5 individuals per team **Task:** Review district- and school-level academic workbooks and respond to the questions.
Analyzing Discipline Data	**Time:** Up to 3 hours for district- and school-level workbooks **Groups:** ~ 4–5 individuals per team **Task:** Review district- and school-level discipline workbooks and respond to the questions.
Intervention Inventory	**Time:** Up to 3 hours **Groups:** ~ 4–5 individuals per team from various grade levels (i.e., elementary, middle, and high school) and different roles **Task:** Complete academic and behavior intervention inventory, including Tiers 1, 2, and 3, and address each question with detailed information. Complete the Gap(s) and Next Steps sections.
Reviewing the Code of Conduct	**Time:** Up to 3 hours (depending on the length and scope of the code of conduct) **Groups:** ~ 4–5 individuals per team with different roles (including parents/caregivers), social identities, and grade levels (i.e., elementary, middle, and high school) **Task:** Read and review the code of conduct and respond to the questions.
Reviewing Discipline Referral Form	**Time:** Up to 3 hours (depending on the number of discipline referral forms) **Groups:** ~ 4–5 individuals per team with different roles (including parents/caregivers), social identities, and grade levels (i.e., elementary, middle and high school). **Task:** Review the discipline referral forms and respond to the questions.

(continued)

Table 4.1. (continued)

Root Cause Phase	Application Task
Analyzing Criteria for AP/ Honors/IB	**Time:** Up to 2 hours
	Groups: ~ 4–5 individuals per team with different roles (including parents/caregivers) and grade levels (i.e., elementary, middle, and high school)
	Task: Review policies connected with AP/Honors, IB, and gifted and talented program enrollment and respond to the questions.
Examining Perspectives on Race and Culture	**Time:** Up to 1 hour
	Groups: ~ 4–5 individuals with different roles per team (including parents/caregivers) and social identities.
	Task: Analyze the survey results and respond to the questions.
Hypothesizing Root Causes of Disproportionality	**Time:** Up to 2 hours
	Groups: ~4–5 individuals with different roles per team (including parents/caregivers), social identities, and grade levels (i.e., elementary, middle, and high school)
	Task: Each team identifies up to 6 root cause hypotheses using evidence from the data, policy, and practice review process.

GARNER CENTRAL SCHOOL DISTRICT: APPLYING A ROOT CAUSE ANALYSIS

Similar to many districts, Garner Central School District (CSD) is a district that in the past decade has seen students and family demographic shifts, particularly growth in their Black, Latinx, and Asian student enrollment. Garner's total student enrollment is 5,656 students. Table 4.2 highlights student enrollment and special classification patterns by race/ ethnicity that have been consistent for the past decade.

Further, in Garner, Latinx students have on average made up 21.01% of the population and their special education classification has remained consistent at 29.90%. Black and Latinx student performance in ELA and math benchmark assessments have consistently been lower in the district in relation to their peers, and they are less likely to be represented in Advanced Placement and Honors classes and in gifted and talented enrollment. Similar to many districts and schools, the racial and ethnic makeup of educators do not reflect the student population. The majority of the educators in Garner are white.

Table 4.2. Garner CSD's Student Enrollment and Special Education Classification

	Enrollment Percentage	Special Education Classification Percentage
Indigenous/Native	0.09%	.12%
Asian	11.23%	7.18%
Black	1.57%	3.48%
Latinx	21.01%	29.90%
White	62.09%	56.78%
Multiracial	3.20%	2.55%

> Your district may have similar patterns to Garner. They may also be different! Make sure to start with a discussion of the student enrollment and special education classification patterns you have in your district.

GROUNDING THE WORK IN A MORAL IMPERATIVE

Moral Imperative Development

Time: Up to 3 hours
Groups: ~ 5 individuals per team
Task: Develop and share personal moral imperatives that ultimately lead to a finalized, group/district moral imperative statement.

One of the critical phases of the root cause analysis process is to develop a moral imperative that serves to lift the importance of the work and to communicate the work to multiple stakeholders. A moral imperative connects individuals to their moral purpose for being in the field of education and builds a deeper understanding of stakeholders' collective moral imperative (Fullan & Quinn, 2016). Further, the moral imperative clarifies for the community what the work is as they move forward, and it offers a roadmap for the "why of the work."

The following is a moral imperative that Garner's district root cause team developed.

The example below demonstrates Garner Central School District's process in developing their moral imperative. Table 4.3 highlights one example of individual moral imperatives written by a team. Table 4.4 depicts the patterns derived from each group's individual moral imperative.

Table 4.3. Example Individual Moral Imperatives, Group 1

As a parent and community leader, I volunteer my time and resources because I feel strongly that every child, every person, deserves the opportunity to succeed without barriers and without biases. Allowing the classroom door to be open for *all* to achieve their fullest potential only opens more doors in the future. It is important for me to address disproportionality because of the role I serve and my ability to take action. I became a board member because I want our students to achieve and have access to excellence, however that may be defined. It is important, and my responsibility in this role, to address disproportionality because achievement and access to excellence can be gained through good governance. Good governance with purposeful action sets the direction and accountability of the district and ultimately can aid in the reduction of barriers and biases.
I want to be one of a cadre of helpers to provide a safe, solid, supportive foundation for children at a crucial point in their development. It is important for me to address disproportionality because *all* children deserve this kind of foundation, regardless of race, ethnicity, gender, socioeconomic situation, etc., and in order for them to get it, there must be a system in place that backs each child and provides them with the resources they need to reach their potential. That system can be built only by addressing/tackling disproportionality wherever it lives.
As a 5th grader, when I wrote an award-winning essay about Dr. King's "I Have a Dream" speech, my instincts about equality were good, but as a white student in a segregated school system in the1960s, I didn't learn the true nature of disproportionality and systemic racism until more recently. Now that I'm in a position to work for systemic change and equity to our district, it is imperative to me that I do so. All children deserve the opportunity to reach their potential. Bias and racism are the root cause of this nation's problems, and our schools are the place we can dismantle disproportionality, teach truth, and bring change.

Table 4.4. Example of Key Moral Imperative Patterns, Group 1

Key Patterns From Moral Imperatives
• Every child, every person, deserves a strong foundation and an opportunity to succeed without barriers and without biases.
• To empower the non-entitled to achieve their dreams
• Need a system in place that backs and supports all students
• Want to improve current conditions
• Provide all students with the necessary resources to reach their fullest potential
• Imperative to bring systemic change to the district

Table 4.5. Key Moral Imperative Words

KEYWORDS: Equity, accountability, potential, access, representation, safe &
supportive, valued, respect, empower, disproportionality, inclusivity, access,
opportunity, advocate, K–12

See the Chapter 4 appendices, Appendix A (https://www.tcpress.com
/filebin/PDFs/9780807769447_app.pdf), for additional moral imperative
examples from Garner that shaped their final statement. Table 4.5 shows
the keywords that were derived from each team's moral imperative patterns. A team developed the moral imperative statement below based on
these keywords (see "Final District Moral Imperative" below).

Final District Moral Imperative

> *At Garner Central School District we believe in the value of all students,
> staff, and families, and the need to eliminate bias and* <u>*disproportionality*</u>
> *in our district and schools. We recognize—and reject—the policies, pro-
> cesses, and systems that create barriers to success. In our schools, race,
> ethnicity, language, culture, gender, sexual orientation, socioeconomic
> status, and learning differences have been barriers and should never be
> predictors of achievement. We are committed to creating a safe, sup-
> portive, and inclusive environment for students, staff, and families; to
> embracing underrepresented voices in our community; and to giving
> every student what they need to achieve their fullest potential at school
> and in life.*

To develop your own collective moral imperative, in teams of 5 individuals, first have each team member craft an individual moral imperative (see
Table 4.6). As individuals develop their moral imperative, they will start
by answering the following questions:

1) Why does equity matter to you in the work you do daily?
2) Why should you address disproportionality?

Once you start developing your district's moral imperative, each individual will read their moral imperative and share why it is important to
them. Once each team member has shared, teams discuss patterns they
heard from group members on their moral imperative and chart them or
type them into a Google Doc or Microsoft Word document that mirrors

Table 4.7. Be prepared to share the patterns you noticed in the larger group. As each team shares, identify a couple of individuals from the whole group to be responsible for taking notes on the patterns they heard across all teams. After hearing the patterns that were captured by the notetakers, individual teams can attempt to draft a 4–5-sentence whole-group statement and then share it, followed by whole-group feedback and final consensus. Smaller groups can skip the individual drafting and just move to whole-group drafting after hearing the patterns.

Table 4.6. Individual Moral Imperative
Write your individual moral imperative on either chart paper or a Google Doc/ Word document.

Table 4.7. Key Patterns From Moral Imperatives
Write key patterns you hear from each team's moral imperative on either chart paper or a Google Doc/Word document.

Patterns	

DISTRICT DATA ANALYSIS

Academic Workbook Analysis Process

As highlighted in Chapter 3, the academic workbook critically examines who is most disproportionately impacted academically. It relies on using common disproportionality calculation methods alongside the disaggregation of data by race/ethnicity, sex, students with an IEP/non-IEP, and the intersectionality of identities (see Chapter 3). Remember, race-conscious data analysis is necessary to identify who is most impacted in the schooling system and specifically to identify and plan to implement targeted change processes. The example academic workbook in Tables 4.8 to 4.13 offers a starting point to help identify academic disparities that exist for students by race/ethnicity. These data were received directly from the district and offer an example of the type of data every school and district should consistently be examining and monitoring for progress. The examples below center on English course pass and failure rates, and AP and Honors enrollment. As stated in Chapter 3, it is important for districts to also use ELA and math benchmark assessments in their data examination.

Table 4.8 shows English course passing and failing rates for grades 6–12 using the three disproportionality calculation methods (see Chapter 3). Follow the outlined tasks in the next sections to practice analyzing the data points from Garner in an effort to build readiness to engage your own data in this same process.

Table 4.8. English (Student Passing and Failing a Course: Grades 6-12)

Race	Racial Composition of Students Who Completed the Course	Composition of Students Passing the Course	Composition of Students Failing the Course	Relative Risk Ratio of Students Passing	Relative Risk Ratio of Students Failing
Indigenous/Native	0.10%	0.00%	1.60%	.51	22.4
Asian	10.60%	10.70%	3.10%	1.02	.27
Black	1.80%	1.60%	9.40%	.90	5.62
Latinx	19.80%	18.80%	60.90%	.94	6.34
White	65.00%	66.00%	21.90%	1.05	.15
Multiracial	2.80%	2.80%	3.10%	1.00	1.11

Task: First review Table 4.8 and take note of patterns you notice. Now complete Table 4.9 to record any disparities you notice. The following is an example of using a data point and focuses on how to apply the composition index: Black students' enrollment in English makes up 1.80% of the overall enrollment of students in English, and their failure in the course is 9.40%.

Table 4.9. English Course Passing/Failing by Race/Ethnicity Findings

What patterns do you notice? What are the disparities?

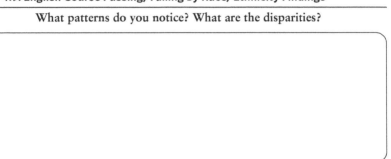

Table 4.10 highlights AP course enrollment by race/ethnicity.

Task: Review Table 4.10 and write down patterns you notice. Now complete Table 4.11 and record any patterns and disparities you notice (e.g., using the composition index, white students make up 62.90% of the district enrollment and their AP enrollment is 71.26%).

Table 4.10. Advanced Placement Course Enrollment by Race/Ethnicity

Race	Racial Composition of School	Composition of Students Enrolled in AP Courses	Risk Index of Enrollment in AP Courses
Indigenous/Native	0.09%	0.00%	0.00%
Asian	11.23%	12.30%	14.81%
Black	1.57%	1.47%	12.64%
Latinx	21.01%	14.17%	9.12%
White	62.90%	71.26%	15.32%
Multiracial	3.20%	.80%	3.39%

Table 4.11. Advanced Placement Enrollment by Race/Ethnicity Findings

What patterns do you notice? What are the disparities?

Table 4.12 highlights enrollment of students in Honors courses by race/ethnicity.

Task: Review Table 4.12 and write down patterns you notice. Now complete Table 4.13 and record any patterns and disparities you notice. The following example demonstrates how to apply the risk index. Using the risk index, Latinx students are enrolled in Honors at 3.53%.

Table 4.12. Honors Course Enrollment by Race/Ethnicity

Race	Racial Composition of School	Composition of Students Enrolled in Honors Courses	Risk Index of enrollment in Honors Courses
Indigenous/Native	0.09%	0.18%	20.00%
Asian	11.23%	13.60%	12.24%
Black	1.57%	.36%	2.30%
Latinx	21.01%	7.33%	3.53%
White	62.90%	77.28%	12.42%
Multi-racial	3.20%	1.25%	3.95%

Table 4.13. Honors Enrollment by Race/Ethnicity Findings

What patterns do you notice? What are the disparities?

Before moving to the discipline and suspension data, use Table 4.14 to record key disparities across all the presented data.

Table 4.14. Key Academic Disparities

Key Disparities
1.
2.
3.
4.

"Look-fors" to not miss while moving through the data:

- Based on the data, regardless of the enrollment size, who is most negatively impacted by the academic programming in this district (and yours)? Did you practice naming this specific disproportionality?
- Who is benefiting the most from academic programming?

Discipline and Suspension Data

Now on to analyzing discipline data. The discipline workbook example in Tables 4.15 to 4.23 offers a guide to identifying discipline disparities that exist for students by race/ethnicity, sex, students with an IEP/non-IEP, and the intersectionality of these identities. The data examples center on the number of students (i.e., students are only counted once) in discipline referrals and suspensions. It is important for districts and schools to track discipline referrals to gain a deeper insight into how the behavior system is impacting disproportionality. What behaviors, and by whom, are leading to referrals and ultimately suspensions? Table 4.15 highlights discipline referrals by race/ethnicity.

> **Task:** Review Table 4.15 and take notes on the patterns you notice. Now complete Table 4.16, writing down patterns and disparities you notice. The following offers an example of how to apply the relative risk ratio (e.g., Black students are 2.62 times more likely to receive a disciplinary referral in comparision to other students).

Table 4.15. Discipline Referrals by Race/Ethnicity

Race	Racial Composition of School	Number of Students Receiving a Disciplinary Referral (students counted only once)	Risk Index of Students Referred (students counted only once)	Relative Risk of Students Referred (students counted only once)
Indigenous/ Native	0.09%	.17%	20.00%	1.93
Asian	11.23%	6.11%	5.64%	.51
Black	1.57%	4.01%	26.44%	2.62
Latinx	21.01%	37.52%	18.50%	2.26
White	62.90%	50.61%	8.34%	.60
Multiracial	3.20%	1.57%	5.08%	.48

Table 4.16. Discipline Referrals by Race/Ethnicity Findings

What patterns do you notice? What are the disparities?

Table 4.17 highlights discipline referrals by race/ethnicity and sex.

Task: Review Table 4.17 and take notes on the patterns you notice. Now complete Table 4.18, writing down patterns and disparities you notice (e.g., using the composition index, Latinx females students make up 21% of the district and are 41.82% of the referrals).

Table 4.17. Discipline Referrals by Race/Ethnicity and Sex

	Indigenous/ Native	Asian	Black	Latinx	White	Multiracial
Composition Female Students Enrolled	0.04%	11.76%	1.85%	21.01%	62.20%	3.14%
Composition Female Students Referred	0.00%	5.45%	7.27%	41.82%	44.24%	1.21%
Risk Index Female Students Referred by Race	0.00%	2.83%	24.00%	12.15%	4.34%	2.35%
Relative Risk of Female Students Referred	0.00	0.43	4.16	2.70	0.48	0.38

(continued)

Table 4.17. (continued)

	Indigenous/ Native	Asian	Black	Latinx	White	Multiracial
Composition Male Students Enrolled	0.14%	10.72%	1.31%	21.01%	63.57%	3.25%
Composition Male Students Referred	0.25%	6.37%	2.70%	35.78%	53.19%	1.72%
Risk Index Male Students Referred by Race	25.00%	8.58%	29.73%	24.58%	12.08%	7.61%
Relative Risk of Male Students Referred	1.73	.57	2.09	2.09	.65	.52

Table 4.18. Discipline Referrals by Race/Ethnicity and Sex Findings

What patterns do you notice? What are the disparities?

Table 4.19 highlights suspensions by race/ethnicity.

Task: Review Table 4.19 and take notes on the patterns you notice. Now complete Table 4.20, recording the patterns and disparities you notice (e.g., using the risk index, white students are suspended at 1.32%).

Table 4.19. Suspensions by Race/Ethnicity

Race	Racial Composition of School	Number of Students Receiving a Suspension (students counted only once)	Risk Index of Students Receiving a Suspension (students counted only once)	Relative Risk of Students Receiving a Suspensions (students counted only once)
Indigenous/ Native	0.09%	0.00%	0.00%	0.00
Asian	11.23%	3.37%	.48%	.28
Black	1.57%	4.49%	4.60%	2.94
Latino/a	21.01%	39.33%	3.01%	2.44
White	62.90%	51.69%	1.32%	.63
Multiracial	3.20%	1.12%	0.56%	.34

Table 4.20. Suspensions by Race/Ethnicity Findings

What patterns do you notice? What are the disparities?

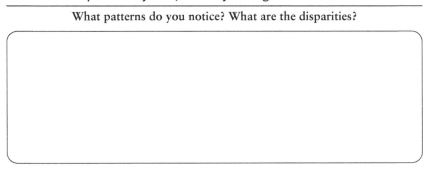

Table 4.21 highlights suspensions by race/ethnicity and sex.

Task: Review Table 4.21 and take notes on the patterns you notice. Now complete Table 4.22, writing down the patterns and disparities you notice (e.g., using the composition index, Black females make up 1.85% of the district and are suspended at 10.71%).

Table 4.21. Suspensions by Race/Ethnicity and Sex

	Indigenous/ Native	Asian	Black	Latinx	White	Multiracial
Composition Female Students Enrolled	0.04%	11.76%	1.85%	21.01%	62.20%	3.14%
Composition Female Students Suspended	0.00%	0.00%	10.71%	35.71%	50.00%	3.57%
Risk Index Female Students Suspended by Race	0.00%	0.00%	6.00%	1.76%	0.83%	1.18%
Relative Risk of Female Students Suspended	0.00	0.00	6.37	2.09	0.61	1.14
Composition Male Students Enrolled	0.14%	10.72%	1.31%	21.01%	63.57%	3.25%
Composition Male Students Suspended	0.00%	4.92%	1.64%	40.98%	52.46%	0.00%
Risk Index Male Students Suspended by Race	0.00%	0.99%	2.70%	4.21%	1.78%	0.00%
Relative Risk of Male Students Suspended	0.00	0.43	1.26	2.61	.63	0.00

Table 4.22. Suspensions by Race/Ethnicity and Sex Findings

What patterns do you notice? What are the disparities?

Before moving on to the next section, use Table 4.23 to document key overall disparities across all the presented data.

Table 4.23. Key Disciplinary Disparities

Key Disparities
1.
2.
3.
4.

"Look-fors" to not miss while moving through the data:

- Based on the data, regardless of the enrollment size, who is most negatively impacted by the behavior pathways in this district (and yours)? Did you practice naming this specific disproportionality?
- Who is least impacted?

EXAMINING KEY POLICIES AND PRACTICES

The data analysis process examples above have allowed you to identify who is most disproportionately impacted academically, and also who disproportionately receives discipline referrals and suspensions. The next step focuses on beginning to examine the academic, behavioral, and social-emotional support systems that exist in a district and a school. These systems can reveal disparate academic and behavior outcomes and experiences. As discussed in Chapter 3, for instance, Tier 1 academics are universally aiming to reach the majority of students and include high-quality, research-based, differentiated instruction; collaborative teaming in general and special education; and data-driven decisions (McIntosh & Goodman, 2016). Ideally, Tier 2 offers targeted intervention supports that address students' specific skill needs on top of Tier 1 instruction. without replacing high-quality, research-based, differentiated instruction and data-driven decision-making. Tier 3 should further increase the intensity of students' targeted intervention, including individualized intervention support, and not replace high-quality, research-based, differentiated instruction and data-driven decision-making (McIntosh & Goodman, 2016).

Chapter 3 described the intervention inventory as a tool to assess the academic and behavioral multitiered systems of support, specifically the type of tiered support offered, how students are referred, how progress of interventions is monitored, the effectiveness of implementation, and the level of cultural responsiveness of each support. Tables 4.24 and 4.25 (academics) and Tables 4.26 and 4.27 (behavior) offer examples of Tiers 1, 2, and 3 academic, behavioral, and social-emotional supports. Educators in Garner were asked the following questions at the top of the tables:

1) What is the name of the intervention?
2) What is the purpose of the intervention?
3) How are students identified for this intervention? What is the frequency and scope of the intervention?
4) When is it offered to students and who is responsible for its delivery?
5) Are the interventions tailored to support the experiences of culturally, racially, and linguistically diverse students?
6) Is the individual implementing the intervention aware of or trained to work with diverse populations?
7) How is the intervention monitored for implementation fidelity?
8) What data are used to assess intervention effectiveness?

Based on Garner's responses, analyze the potential gaps and next steps in their district. Using the blank template in Appendix K from the Chapter 3 appendices (https://www.tcpress.com/filebin/PDFs/9780807769447_app .pdf), follow the same process for your own district.

Task: First review Tables 4.24 and 4.25 for academics, and then address the following questions in Table 4.26: (1) What are the gaps you noticed in the academic Tiers 1, 2, and 3 intervention and supports? (2) What potential academic Tiers 1, 2, and 3 interventions and supports are missing? (3) What could be the next steps?

Table 4.24. Tier 1 Academic Intervention and Supports

Name of intervention	What is the purpose of the intervention?	How are students identified for this intervention? What is the frequency and scope of the intervention?	When is it offered to students and who is responsible for its delivery?	Are the interventions tailored to support the experiences of culturally, racially, and linguistically diverse students?	Is the individual implementing the intervention aware of or trained to work with diverse populations?	How is the intervention monitored for implementation fidelity?	What data are used to assess intervention effectiveness?
Guided Reading	Leveled Literacy Intervention Program	All students receive this intervention. Levels are determined by Fountas & Pinnell.	During the students' reading time in class, and the classroom teacher delivers it.	Marginal. ENL* teachers are partnered as co-teachers in homerooms. Tailored linguistically because ENL students will often be in a group together.	Limited to none	School-wide data. Classroom data. Benchmarking of Fountas and Pinnell. Progress monitoring 6 weeks	Fountas and Pinnell[1]. STAR. Teacher's knowledge of the child
Small group writing	Writing support	Teacher's College writing. Frequency and scope determined by teacher/teacher knowledge	During students' writing time in class, and the classroom teacher delivers it.	Marginally to none. ENL teachers are partnered as co-teachers in homerooms.	Limited to none	Teachers College running records. Teacher's informal assessment/impressions of students' abilities	Student work
Small group reteaching	Math	Frequency and scope determined by teacher/teacher knowledge/student need	During the students' math time in class and the classroom; teacher delivers it.	Tailored linguistically because ENL students will often be in a group together with similar needs.	Limited to none	Teacher's informal assessment/impressions of students' abilities	Student work

*ENL stands for English as a New Language

Table 4.25. Tier 2 and 3 Academic Intervention and Supports

Name of intervention name	What is the purpose of the intervention?	How are students identified for this intervention? What is the frequency and scope of the intervention?	When is it offered to students and who is responsible for its delivery?	Are the interventions tailored to support the experiences of culturally, racially, and linguistically diverse students?	Is the individual implementing the intervention aware of or trained to work with diverse populations?	How is the intervention monitored for implementation fidelity?	What data are used to assess intervention effectiveness?
Fountas and Pinnell: Leveled Literacy Intervention- Tier 2/3	Decoding Comprehension Fluency	STAR* data when students perform in the red and yellow levels Cross-checked with Fountas and Pinnell score 2 or 3 times a week for 25 minutes at a time (Usually it is 5 times a week for 30 minutes)	Offered by semester Reading specialists are responsible.	Marginal to none; tailored linguistically because ENL students will often be in a group together with similar needs. *If a child is marked for intervention and they are ENL, they go to the ENL specialist first.	Marginally to none	Reading specialists have been trained to deliver the literacy intervention Ongoing professional development Common planning time K–2 and K–5 Reading liaison who is in charge of it all	Benchmarking Progress monitoring

RTI** Math	Basic math skills Computation/number sense/place value	First- and 2nd-grade students who have STAR* data who perform in the red and yellow levels	Offered by semester Math specialists are responsible.	Marginal to not at all tailored linguistically because ENL students will often be in a group together with similar needs.	Marginally to none	Ongoing professional development Common planning time	Progress monitoring Benchmarking
Fast-ForWord	Pre-reader Letter sounds letter names Works better for ENL population	Students who aren't ready for literacy intervention	Throughout the school year through reading specialist or teacher assistant (small group) Currently 2–3 times a week . . . normally 5 days a week for 30 minutes	Marginal to none	Teachers are trained	There is only one person who delivers this intervention Ongoing professional development	Built into the program because it is computer-based and progressive.

*STAR is a Standardized Test for the Assessment of Reading

**RTI in Math stands for Response to Intervention in Mathematics

Table 4.26. Academics Intervention and Supports Gaps

What are the gaps you noticed in the academic Tiers 1, 2, and 3 interventions and supports?	
What potential academic Tiers 1, 2, and 3 interventions and supports are missing?	
What are potential next steps?	

Task: First review Table 4.27 and Table 4.28 for behavior and social-emotional supports and then respond to the questions in Table 4.29: (1) What are the gaps you noticed in the behavioral and social-emotional Tiers 1, 2, and 3 interventions and supports? (2) What potential behavioral and social-emotional Tiers 1, 2, and 3 interventions and supports are missing? (3) What are potential next steps?

Table 4.27. Tier 1 Behavior and Social-Emotional Intervention and Supports

Name of intervention	What is the purpose of the intervention?	How are students identified for this intervention? What is the frequency and scope of the intervention?	When is it offered to students and who is responsible for its delivery?	Are the interventions tailored to support the experiences of culturally, racially, and linguistically diverse students?	Is the individual implementing the intervention aware of or trained to work with diverse populations?	How is the intervention monitored for implementation fidelity?	What data are used to assess intervention effectiveness?
Morning meetings	Establish relationships among students and teachers/community-building	Daily—whole class	Daily—homeroom teacher(s)	No	No	It's not	No data are collected.
Social-emotional classroom lessons with school counselor	Increase social-emotional intelligence. Provide students with strategies/tools for emotional/academic success	Whole class, minimum three times a year.	3 times a year with school counselor	No	Yes	Delivered by same staff member to all classes	Not yet
Classroom PBIS systems	To reinforce positive behavior and behavioral expectations	Daily basis—whole class	Daily homeroom teachers	No	Yes	No	No data are collected.

Table 4.28. Tier 2 Behavioral and Social-Emotional Intervention and Supports

Intervention name	What is the purpose of the intervention?	How are students identified for this intervention? What is the frequency and scope of the intervention?	When is it offered to students and who is responsible for its delivery?	Are the interventions tailored to support the experiences of culturally, racially, and linguistically diverse students?	Is the individual implementing the intervention aware of or trained to work with diverse populations?	How is the intervention monitored for implementation fidelity?	What data are used to assess intervention effectiveness?
Attendance letters/calls/visits	Address attendance issues—get kids to consistently attend	Review of attendance data/monthly	Students with greater than 10 absences per review cycle—assistant principal	Varies	Varies	Monthly attendance meetings	Overall attendance data/length of engagement time for remote students
Building-level counseling	To address behaviors that are impeding academic success	Teachers/referrals Duration varies depending on students' needs	School counselor Social worker School psychologist	Yes Bilingual school counselor	Yes	Goals/purpose are set at the beginning of counseling. Duration is adjusted based on the needs of the group/individual.	Teacher feedback

Tier 3 Behavioral and Social-Emotional Intervention and Supports

Individual behavior plans (formal and informal)	Address specific student need within the classroom	Teacher feedback/data and observation	Classroom teachers	Varies	Varies	Data collection	Overall data collection of attempts/successes

Table 4.29. Behavioral and Social-Emotional Intervention Supports Gaps

What are the gaps you noticed in the behavior and social-emotional Tiers 1, 2, and 3 intervention and supports?	
What potential behavior and social-emotional Tiers 1, 2, and 3 interventions and supports are missing?	
What are potential next steps?	

POLICY AND PRACTICE: CODE OF CONDUCT AND DISCIPLINE REFERRAL FORM EXAMPLES AND ADVANCED PLACEMENT, HONORS, INTERNATIONAL BACCALAUREATE, AND GIFTED AND TALENTED FORM

Code of Conduct

As highlighted in Chapter 3, one of the central policies that is examined during the root cause process is a district's code of conduct. This is done to assess how the language in policies may be leading to disproportionate discipline referrals and suspensions. The example below shows an analysis of Garner CSD's code of conduct, in which their root cause team reviewed and answered the questions in Table 4.30. We understand that this example may not be comprehensive; nonetheless, the purpose is to use the analysis as a practice application to then analyze your district's code of conduct; in Garner, 4–5 individuals from the root cause community with different roles, social identities, and grade levels (i.e., elementary, middle, and high school) reviewed the code of conduct. Parents/caregivers are part of this team. The team should be given ample time to review the code of conduct (in our experience, a half to a full day is necessary, depending on the length and scope of the code of conduct).

> **Task:** First, review Table 4.30 to take note of patterns from Garner CSD's code of conduct analysis. In Table 4.31 address the following: (1) What are the gaps? (2) What are potential next steps?

Table 4.30. Garner CSD Code of Conduct Analysis

How does the code of conduct align with your overall district culture and mission?	The code of conduct does not align in terms of creating a partnership between school and families. The code and mission are broad and appear aligned, but the exceptions to how the code of conduct is not aligned to the mission are the dress code, sexual identity categories, electronic devices, and social media platforms. The code of conduct includes student rights and responsibilities, parent rights and responsibilities, teachers/staff/ administration rights and responsibilities.
How was the code of conduct created?	The code was created by the previous Board of Education (BOE), along with district attorneys. At the policy meeting, community comments were taken and disseminated to the community. The code of conduct was last revised in 2015.
Was there parent, student, and community involvement in the creation of the code of conduct?	There was a collaborative approach among board members, administrators, and attorneys. Parents were not part of the process, nor were students and teachers (meetings were during the school day). There was no formal committee for community feedback, but comments were invited by the Board.
How often is the code of conduct revised? Who is involved in making the revisions to the code of conduct?	It was last revised 6 years ago. The revision of the code of conduct is made by BOE's Policy and Personnel Committee and includes an administrator.

Table 4.30 (*continued*)

What is the purpose of the code of conduct?	The purpose of the code of conduct is to provide expectations of how students, staff, BOE, visitors, and community members should act while on (and off) school grounds and during school activities and events.
What are the goals of the code of conduct?	The goals of the code of conduct are to: (a) ensure a safe learning environment for the school community; (b) provide a common language and understanding as to how to maintain a safe environment conducive to learning; (c) make students, staff, etc. aware of rights and responsibilities and consequences thereof; and (d) provide protection for all persons within the district. *There is space for interpretation in the code of conduct.
Does the code of conduct consider how culture shapes variation in behavior?	The code of conduct doesn't reference culture. It presumes everyone is the same. The Consequence section does speak to age, disciplinary record, information from parents, and extenuating circumstances. *This section would be a good place to add in language about cultural variation in behaviors.*
How does the code of conduct move past punishment and into support?	The code of conduct does have language on moving from punishment into support, and the Remedial Measure section addresses peer support groups, corrective instruction or other relevant help, supportive intervention, behavior management plans, student counseling, and parent conferences. It is unclear if it is implemented as intended.
Does the code of conduct move away from exclusionary discipline and use suspension as a last resort?	The code of conduct lists many disciplinary actions to take prior to suspending a student. Suspension should be avoided and used as a last resort. It is unclear if these steps are followed equitably for all students.
Is there a progressive ladder of support embedded into the code of conduct and aligned to the disciplinary responses?	There is a progression outlined in the code of conduct, but we don't have data to analyze whether it is followed.

(*continued*)

Table 4.30 (continued)

For each infraction, is there a range of possible discipline responses that can be used?	Yes, there is a range of discipline responses, including peer support groups; behavioral assessment/evaluation; student counseling and parent/caregiver counseling; verbal warnings detention; suspension from transportation; suspension from athletic participation, extracurricular activities, and other privileges; in-school suspensions; teacher disciplinary removal of disruptive students; short-term (5 days or less) suspension from school; and long-term (more than 5 days) suspension from school. It is not clear what discipline infraction leads to what discipline response.
Does the code of conduct make space for restoration and relationship-building?	Yes, there is a sense of using peer mediation groups. There is inconsistent application. More restorative practices and relationship building is needed. There should be less exclusionary practices.
How does your school use the code of conduct? How is it used by teachers? How is it used by school administrators?	Teachers use the code of conduct when they see something wrong; they call the assistant principal, get a statement, and then they take care of it. They don't refer to the code regularly. The code defines expectations for the students and the assistant principal operationalizes it. Teachers mainly rely on discussions with students about good/bad choices. They take care of 90% of behaviors on their own. The code of conduct is used as a reference point used by administrators. It is utilized by administrators depending on the circumstances of the situation. It doesn't seem to be used by teachers and parents at all until there is a disciplinary situation.
How does your school ensure that all staff members have the same understanding of the code of conduct?	The code of conduct is available to anyone. It is published on the district website.
How do students and families receive the code of conduct?	The code of conduct is posted on the website, and the families receive a letter with a link to the code of conduct at the start of the school year.
How does your school ensure that every student understands the code of conduct?	Overall, it is unclear how the code of conduct is communicated to students and if it requires a signature. At the high school the code of conduct is discussed in grade-level assemblies at the beginning of each school year.

Table 4.30 (*continued*)

What ambiguous language or language that is open to interpretation exists in the code of conduct?	There are areas of ambiguous language in the code of conduct, including disruptive, insubordinate, and disrespectful. Disruptiveness can range from running in halls to computer/electronic communications misuse, including any unauthorized use of computers, software, or Internet/intranet accounts; accessing inappropriate websites; or any other violation of the district's acceptable use policy.
	Insubordinate behavior can range from failing to comply with the reasonable directions of teachers, school administrators, or other school employees in charge of students or otherwise demonstrating disrespect, to lateness.
Is there language in the code of conduct that leads to criminalizing students?	Yes, *juvenile delinquent*, *juvenile offender*, and *violent student* appear in the code of conduct.
Does the code of conduct reflect age-appropriate responses to discipline?	The code of conduct does discuss how age should be a factor when determining disciplinary measures; this area needs to be made more explicit.
Does the code of conduct include relevant protections from state and federal laws on the rights of students with disabilities and the responsibilities of the school in these cases?	Yes, the code of conduct has a section on manifestation hearings and disciplinary actions for students with IEPs.
Does the code of conduct clearly spell out due process, including a process of appealing suspensions?	Yes, when there is a superintendent hearing an appeal can be made to the Board. But there is a question as to how the appeal is received and by which students. To that end, the process needs to be clearer.
Does the code of conduct clearly indicate under what conditions law enforcement may become involved?	Yes; however, we tend not to go to law enforcement as a practice.

(*continued*)

Table 4.30 (*continued*)

Does the code of conduct allow discretion to be used in consequences on a case-by-case basis?	Yes, the code of conduct allows for discretion in consequences dependent on the incident.
Does the code of conduct clearly spell out what can lead to detention, ISS, and OSS? And the number of days of detention, ISS, and OSS? Provide examples.	No, the code of conduct does not say which infractions lead to which outcomes. As for number of days, the code discusses the difference in procedure for over 5 days of OSS and under 5 days of OSS.

Table 4.31. Code of Conduct Analysis Gaps and Next Steps

What are some gaps?	
What are potential next steps?	

Discipline Referral Form

Analyzing a school/district's discipline referral form is the next step after the code of conduct analysis. The discipline referral form analysis reveals the way the code of conduct is operating within schools and classrooms.

That is, you get a sense of the overall utility of the discipline referral form and, most importantly, the impact on students. How are discipline incidents being documented? What decisions are school staff making on potential disciplinary outcomes? The purpose of this process is for your team to review Garner's analysis of their referral form and identify gaps and next steps. When your team analyzes the discipline referral form(s), identify a separate team of 4–5 individuals from within the larger root cause team—including parents/caregivers, and school and district staff from the elementary, middle, and high schools—to review the form(s). Make sure all discipline referral form(s) have been collected from all schools before the analysis. It is also important here to offer ample time for the team to review the discipline referral forms and address the questions in Table 4.32.

> **Task:** First, review the Garner CSD discipline referral analysis in Table 4.32. Take notes as you review the response to the questions, and then address the following questions in Table 4.33: (1) What are the gaps? (2) What are potential next steps?

Table 4.32. Garner CSD Discipline Referral Analysis

What is the purpose of the discipline referral form?	At the elementary school, the referral form is used for recordkeeping.
	At the middle school, the form appears to have the opportunity for students to reflect on their behavior. It allows the student to calm down before engaging in a conversation. Another purpose of the referral form at the middle school is streamlined communication between a teacher and an administrator. That is, the purpose of the staff form is to gain assistance in handling a student's behavior. The student contact form is for students to report an incident.
When is this form used?	At the elementary level, the form is used for keeping track of how many times a behavior incident occurred. However, it is not necessarily completed every time a student has a behavior incident.
	At the middle school, the form is used to streamline communication between a teacher and an administrator and for secondary-level recordkeeping. The staff form is used when a teacher has exhausted all the steps they would typically use to address an

(continued)

Table 4.32 (continued)

	issue; it is used as a last resort. The use of the form is dependent on the degree of the infraction, and a form may not always be required. The student contact form is used when a student goes to an assistant principal to report a student or situation. The student is looking for assistance, and it is a way to document the information.
How does your school use this form? How is it used by teachers, and how is it used by school administrators? When are teachers and staff trained on the purpose and use of this form?	**By teachers:** The form is used by teachers or paraprofessionals who witness an incident and it is beyond what they can handle and so they give it to the principal. The principal determines who to include and what action is needed, and whether a Dignity for All Students Act (DASA) action is warranted.[2] At the elementary level, the form may never be filled out, but, rather, students are dropped off in the principal's office. **By administrators:** The principals use the form to determine the course of action that needs to be taken. At the middle school, the staff can access the form online or request a hard copy from the office. The assistant principal uses the form as a starting point for conversations with a student. An investigation may ensue, and the form is used as documentation. Teachers and staff are not trained on the discipline referral forms.
What are the possible outcomes when this form is used?	The high school form looks punitive and has no option for behavioral intervention. Two of the elementary forms have space for further action and follow-up on what actions were taken. At the middle school, the administrator may ask for clarification. The assistant principal will speak to the student or investigate the situation. This may result in disciplinary action—a warning or maybe lunch detention, an ISS, or a guidance referral and parent discussion.
When is the form entered into a data system?	The form is not entered in the data system at this time at the elementary level. At the middle school, the clerical staff enters the data into a data system after the infraction. The teachers are notified when student referrals are entered.

Table 4.32 (*continued*)

Do the behavior infractions and consequences in the form align with the code of conduct?	The Board of Education code of conduct is broad but provides little guidance. At the middle school, the behavior incidents and consequences align with the code of conduct. The code of conduct is far more specific than the referral form. The Reason for Referral section on the form is more general in the purpose.
What ambiguous language or language that is open to interpretation exists in this form?	The high school form is punitive in its language, including reprimand, detention, ISS, OSS, and in-school detention. The language for the title of the form should be an incident referral instead of a disciplinary referral. The middle school form includes "inappropriate actions" as possibly culturally insensitive and ambiguous. The use of "disrespectful" is ambiguous because it is based on the subjective opinions of the person issuing the referral. "Insubordination" also appears on the form. On the form, Steps Taken Prior to the Referral makes it seem like a form is completed for students with multiple referrals. The Reason for Referral section isn't specific on the form.
Does the form include space to list interventions/supports that have been offered to students to address behavior?	The elementary form does have a space to include interventions and supports. In the middle school form, there are only steps the teacher has taken but no area that indicates intervention or supports that were used.
Does the form require that administrators, teachers, and staff include student demographic information (i.e., race, ethnicity, gender, IEP/non-IEP status)?	The form does not collect demographic information other than the student's name because the data are entered into the system that already lists the student's race, ethnicity, gender, and IEP/non-IEP status. However, if the demographic information was included, it requires staff to be more cognizant of the information by adding a place to include intervention on the form. This may provide more specific, related strategies for the particular student.

Table 4.33. Discipline Referral Form Gaps and Next Steps

What are some gaps?	
What are potential steps?	

Additionally, districts should consider analyzing policies and practices around AP/Honors/IB enrollment, as well as criteria for students to qualify for gifted and talented programs. More often than not, the policies and practices associated with AP/Honors/IB enrollment and gifted and talented programs impact which students are represented in enrollment. It is recommended that when your district moves through the root cause analysis that you engage in this process.

Task: First, gather policies, procedures, and practices for AP/Honors/IB enrollment and gifted and talented programs. In teams of 4–5, review the policies, procedures, and practices. Make sure to take notes on what the team is noticing. Respond to the questions in Table 4.34 to analyze your district's AP, Honors, and IB enrollment policies and practices. Respond to the questions in Table 4.35 to analyze your district's gifted and talented policies and practices.

Table 4.34. Advanced Placement, Honors, and IB Enrollment Analysis

What is the criterion for AP/Honors/IB enrollment?	AP:
	Honors:
	IB:
Can students enroll in AP/Honors/IB even when they are not on this track?	AP:
	Honors:
	IB:
How are final decisions made about who ends up enrolled in AP/Honors/IB?	AP:
	Honors:
	IB:

(*continued*)

Table 4.34 (*continued*)

What are the gaps?	
What are the next steps?	

Table 4.35. Gifted and Talented Enrollment Criterion

What is the criterion for gifted and talented enrollment?	
What assessments are used to determine gifted and talented enrollment? How are the assessments fair to students of color and multilingual learners?	Assessment used:
	Assessment and fairness:

Table 4.35 (continued)

Can students enroll in gifted and talented at any grade?	
How are final decisions made about who ends up enrolled in gifted and talented enrollment?	
What are the gaps?	
What are the next steps?	

EXAMINING STAFF BELIEFS

In the root cause analysis, district and school staff complete a survey that examines their beliefs. For over a decade, we have used the Perspectives on Race and Culture survey based on the diversity scale developed by Russell Skiba and others at the Indiana University Equity Project. The modified scale has five subscales that measure perceptions on student success, color evasiveness, racial awareness and knowledge, professional responsibility, and deficit thinking (Valencia, 1997) about students from racially, culturally, and linguistically diverse backgrounds (see Appendix B, Chapter 4 appendices [https://www.tcpress.com/filebin/PDFs/9780807769447_app .pdf] for subscale questions). The Likert scale response options range from "1–strongly disagree" to "6–strongly agree." Figure 4.1 highlights aggregate scores from Garner's survey results. A higher score in the sub-scales of Ensuring Student Success and Professional Responsibility indicates higher levels of educators' commitment to student success and a sense of professional responsibility, respectively. Overall, a lower score in the Color-Evasiveness subscale designates lower levels of color-evasiveness (i.e., more prone to being color-conscious). A lower score in the Racial Awareness and Knowledge subscale means less racial awareness and knowledge. A higher score in the Deficit Thinking about Students subscale indicates higher levels of deficit thinking.

In thinking about the root cause analysis process in your district, seek out external support to survey staff members to identify and analyze the beliefs held in the community. That includes (a) identifying who can create the online survey, (b) how it will be distributed and communicated district-wide to all staff, (c) who will conduct that analysis and create a report, and (d) how it will be analyzed in the root cause team and shared district- and school-wide.

> **Task:** First, review Figure 4.1, take notes on the patterns you notice, and then answer the questions in Table 4.36.

Figure 4.1. Staff Perspective on Culture and Race Aggregate Scores

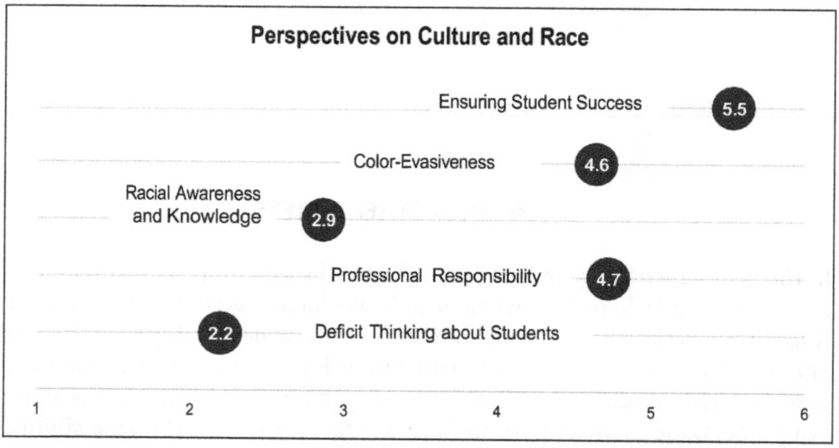

The Ensuring Student Success, Color-Evasiveness, Racial Awareness and Knowledge, Deficit Thinking, and Professional Responsibility scales are measured on a scale of 1 to 6, with 1 being Strongly Disagree and 6 being Strongly Agree. A higher score reflects a higher level of agreement. A lower score reflects a lower level of agreement.

Table 4.36. Perspectives on Race and Culture Analysis

What patterns do you notice in the survey results?	
What do the data suggest?	

GETTING TO ROOT CAUSES

Root Cause Hypothesis

Now that you have moved through some example academic and behavioral student outcomes and policies, practices, and beliefs connected to them, what are potential root causes that you are noticing? Complete Table 4.37 to identify potential root cause hypotheses leading to Garner's disproportionality. Hypotheses are possible explanations for what is shaping disproportionality. Team members should be in groups of 4–5. Each group engages in a dialogue about what is leading to the disproportionality in the district given the data; conversations held during the sessions; and policy, procedures, and practice reviews. See Chapter 4 appendices, Appendix C (https://www.tcpress.com/filebin/PDFs/9780807769447_app.pdf), for examples of root causes and the connected beliefs, policies, and practices.

Here are guiding questions to support the development of aligned root cause hypotheses:

- What specific evidence do you have connecting the hypothesis to the data analysis process? For example, if you say "professional development on biases and deficit thinking" is a root cause of

Table 4.37. Root Cause Hypotheses

Hypothesis:	BPPPs Connected to Hypothesis:
1.	Beliefs:
	Policies:
	Procedures/Practices:
2.	Beliefs:
	Policies:
	Procedures/Practices:
3.	Beliefs:
	Policies:
	Procedures/Practices:
4.	Beliefs:
	Policies:
	Procedures/Practices:
5.	Beliefs:
	Policies:
	Procedures/Practices:

disproportionality, does the Perspectives on Race and Culture
survey highlight this need? Did these beliefs come out during
parent/caregiver and student focus groups, or elsewhere in the
analysis process?
- Does your hypothesis for a root cause to disproportionality
  directly respond to the communities that are most impacted? For
  example, if "inconsistent Tiers 2 and 3 behavior interventions"
  is your proposed root cause, do training and development in
  this directly improve outcomes and experiences for the students
  most disproportionately impacted? Take a look again at your
  disproportionality data. Who is most impacted, and how will
  this particular community benefit from tackling the above root
  cause?
- Can you name the beliefs, policies, practices, and procedures
  connected to your proposed root cause? Disproportionality is
  maintained through BPPPs, so effective improvement to a root
  cause issue means actively interrogating the BPPPs that uphold
  the disproportionality.

Based on the review of the process documents shared, add root cause hypotheses connected to the disproportionality in Garner (e.g., inconsistency
in application of the code of conduct; lacking strong Tier 1 support academics; lack of usage of data to inform instruction, biases, and racism;
etc.). From these hypotheses, the root cause team selects no more than 5
focus areas to move with into action planning. We generally recommend 3
to 4 focus areas depending on the district. It is critical that teams make sure
the selected focus areas are fully backed by evidence from the root cause
analysis process. When carrying out your own root cause analysis, there
will be a curated team for each of the focus areas. Select these teams based
on their role and the experience they bring to the particular focus area.
Individual teams then develop action plans specific to their focus area.

The Root Cause Analysis Profile

The profile template in Table 4.38 highlights sections from each part of
the root cause process. The aim is for your team to use the profile once
you complete the root cause processes. We recommend that for practice,
you first fill out the profile using the data you have moved through from
our sample district, Garner. Next, and most importantly, use the framing
provided here to enter the outcomes of each of the root cause sections
your team inevitably moves through with your own district data.

The profile serves to name the gaps and propel an active response to
the inequities uncovered during the root cause process. It also operates

Table 4.38. Root Cause Analysis Profile

ROOT CAUSE ANALYSIS PROFILE *In the spaces below, list the most important pieces of each key root cause area.*	
Moral imperative:	
Voices of those most impacted: *Highlight any parent/caregiver and student focus group quotes here, particularly from voices who have been disproportionately impacted. See Chapter 3 for more information about focus groups.*	
Academic/discipline key data points:	
Intervention inventory gaps:	
Code of conduct gaps:	
Discipline referral gaps:	
Identified focus areas based on the hypotheses of root causes: *What are the areas in need of improvement that can most impact the inequities uncovered in the analysis process (e.g., family engagement, Tier 1 culturally responsive interventions, multitiered system of supports)?*	

as a messaging tool—offering clear and coherent takeaways that explain why moving toward equity is crucial. This profile will support how teams then engage in action planning. Identifying the disproportionality within a district is a foundational first step, but without a well-developed plan for dismantling the inequities that currently exist, districts will fail to shift toward equity for every student. To that end, the next steps are outlining a detailed action planning process.

ACTION PLANNING AFTER A ROOT CAUSE ANALYSIS

We have witnessed countless district teams become very motivated in the process of uncovering the inequities that exist in their district, courageously naming the elephants in the room, only to be met with apathy, reluctance, or even fear to take the next step for systemic change. The racial equity tensions we talked through in Chapter 1 become deeply embedded during these moments of *"what's next?"* From individuals exemplifying a lack of personal readiness to a lagging systemic influence, often embodied by a superintendent or a board member, progress is often met with pushback. In trainings, we stress the need for "teeth" attached to the root cause process. How will the critical work attach to the DNA of the district in order for the needed change to continue? Strategic, coherent, multiyear action planning becomes critical, distinctly different from the watered-down versions of diversity, inclusion, and equity (DEI) initiatives that often get thrown in the mix with the district's overall strategic plan. Districts need action plans that are directly tied to the root cause analysis process; they need responses, pathways, to fill the gaps that were uncovered. For additional clarity, here are a few key points for the team to take with them into the action planning process:

1. Center those most impacted by disproportionality—action planning only matters if you continue to name the elephants in the room and create action steps directly responding to the disproportionality data uncovered during the root cause analysis process. Continue to *focus on students and families who are relegated to the margins,* recognizing that if we meet the needs of the communities most impacted, everyone will benefit. This looks like not hiding from or explaining away the data or the experiences our Black, Indigenous, and students of color are sharing, but rather leaning into believing and actively responding to the data and narratives.
2. Your action plan has to have teeth—S.M.A.R.T. (specific, measurable, achievable, relevant, and time-bound) goals and

implementation strategies ensure active next steps. Be as specific as possible to outline these multiyear actions.

3. Make the action plan institutional, not individual—your plan shouldn't simply rely on just certain people, but rather operate as an institutional document others can follow and be motivated to support. When inevitable staffing changes occur, the plan should still remain and be accessible to others.

Lastly, we recommend that teams review the reading *Four Domains for Rapid School Improvement: An Implementation Framework* (Jackson et al., 2018) that is listed in pre–root cause analysis readings in the Chapter 3 appendices, Appendix C (https://www.tcpress.com/filebin/PDFs /9780807769447_app.pdf). This grounding will further support your team's effective implementation.

Components of an Effective Action Plan

Focus Area(s). Throughout the root cause analysis process, teams gather quantitative and qualitative data and inevitably start making connections to the potential root causes for the disproportionality that exists within the district. From this analysis, teams need to pick up to 5 focus areas that are directly connected to the root causes discussed. For example, after moving through all of the processes outlined in this chapter, districts often realize that their multitiered system of supports (MTSS) does not adequately meet the needs of their student population. More specifically, behavioral and academic interventions are not culturally responsive; they often are actually destructive, compliance/punishment-based, and exclusive to white normative cultural expectations. MTSS becomes a key entry point and root cause of disproportionality and a key opening for developing robust, equity-based interventions. The action plan example we offer in Table 4.39 outlines how a district created steps to strengthen their MTSS.

Other focus areas that often arise as having critical gaps that lead to root causes for disproportionality are:

- Family/community engagement
- Professional development
- Teaching and learning

That said, the focus areas chosen by the team need to be directly aligned with the root cause analysis findings and specific needs of the district's student and family community.

Culturally Responsive Usable Practice. The Usable Practice statement is a clear description of what the intended change will be to the focus

Table 4.39. Action Plan Example

Focus Area:

Multitiered System of Supports (MTSS)

Culturally Responsive Usable Practice:

Develop and implement an MTSS that is culturally responsive to racially, culturally, and linguistically marginalized students to inform data-driven decision-making and provide culturally responsive tiered supports to shift inequitable discipline and academic outcomes.

Year 1	Year 2	Year 3	Year 4	Year 5
Outcome Goal:	Outcome Goal:	Outcome Goal:	Outcome Goal:	Outcome Goal:
By June 2024, Tier 1 behavioral MTSS will be reviewed and revised.	By June 2025, 100% of staff will know how to use the Tier 1 culturally responsive MTSS, including code of character, conduct and support, a revised plan for social-emotional learning, and restorative practices.	By June 2026, there will be a 25% reduction of behavioral referrals for Black, multiracial, and Latinx students.	By June 2027, there will be a 50% reduction of behavioral referrals for Black, multiracial, and Latinx students.	By June 2028, there will be a 75% reduction of behavioral referrals for Black, multiracial, and Latinx students.

area identified. It is critical that this statement be grounded in cultural responsiveness, meaning that it clearly looks to shift the focus area toward equity for students most impacted. For instance, the culturally responsive usable practice for an MTSS focus area could be (as identified in the example): *Develop and implement a multitiered system of supports (MTSS) that is culturally responsive to racially, culturally, and linguistically marginalized students to inform data-driven decision-making and provide culturally responsive tiered supports to shift inequitable discipline and academic outcomes.* The process that would ultimately lead to this usable practice being effectively implemented would include several tiered steps like (but not limited to): (1) analyzing the current discipline processes and revising behavioral policies that have led to disproportionate referrals and suspensions of students of color, and (2) developing a plan for training and implementation of a more restorative approach to school culture. As policies and practices shift, it will be critical that there be a mechanism to assess whether the usable practice is being implemented effectively. In the above example of a usable MTSS culturally responsive practice, this could look like an ongoing analysis of disaggregated suspension and referral data to ensure there is less disproportionality. As you will see in the example plan, the usable practice should be consistent for all years of the action plan. That is, the year 1 implementation should have the same overarching usable practice as years 2 and 3.

Outcome Goal. It is important to identify outcome goals for each year of the multiyear plan. Outcome goals center on what will be accomplished in a given year. These time-bound annual goals keep teams on task to move toward long-term systemic change. As you will see, there are often multiple smaller "S.M.A.R.T. goals" within the year that will ensure the outcome goal is met.

S.M.A.R.T. Goal(s). A quick note on S.M.A.R.T. goals, as we have worked with several districts where educators have not received training in developing goals that are "S.M.A.R.T." As you will see in the example plan, within each implementation year, there will be incremental goals that the implementation team will need to execute to reach each annual outcome goal. Each goal should be Specific, Measurable, Achievable, Relevant, and Time-bound. We have noticed that measurability and having a time frame are paramount. Often S.M.A.R.T. goals start with "By [month], [year], we will . . . The action planning team must then clarify the feasibility of the goal (whether it is achievable), making sure that within the district's current structure it is possible to successfully accomplish and that they know what "meeting the goal" looks like (measurability).

EXAMPLE S.M.A.R.T. GOAL:

By June 2020, review and revise the Code of Character, Conduct, and Support to assess inclusive language and processes for racially, culturally, and linguistically marginalized students and families.

Implementation Phases. In order to meet and sustain the outlined usable practice, certain phases must be reached. As schools and districts develop their multiyear action plans, it is important to think about the current phase of implementation. Often, a district will identify a root cause for disproportionality and a focus area that is connected to work that has already started. For example, with an MTSS focus area, a code of conduct review may have already been a part of the district's annual strategic plan (before the root cause analysis)—they may have already picked a team; the team may have even met and started to move through the revisions. That said, when identifying the code of conduct review as a critical part of the new action plan process, it will not be at the "exploration phase" but rather potentially at the "installation" or even "initial implementation" phase. With this in mind, teams still have to honestly assess whether the work already done has been engaged with an equity/culturally responsive lens. If not, then reengaging the existing team with this training and support is critical. More details on the four phases of implementation follow:

Exploration: This becomes the first year of creating readiness to engage systems change. In this year of exploration, districts must think about (a) defining selection criteria for team members, roles, and responsibilities; (b) developing a vision for the usable practice; and (c) identifying the particular practice that will be engaged. Districts often look to jump into change without addressing their readiness, which inevitably impacts the potential for sustained change.

Installation: This phase focuses on assembling human and financial resources. In this stage, the implementation team and school and district leaders are preparing for initiating the practices outlined in the exploration phase. This includes preparing training sessions, creating assessment materials, recruiting the first cohort of leaders and staff, and meeting with key stakeholders to message the work.

Initial Implementation: During this phase, the work of the outlined change has started to occur. This can look like the completion of training with the first cohort of leaders and staff. Coaching is occurring (if needed) and is occurring frequently. One central goal of this phase is to assure that the practice that everyone was trained and coached on is occurring. That is, is the training that school and district leaders started to implement beginning to meet their identified need?

Full implementation: This takes 3 to 5 years to achieve. With equity work, we have found that this process can take even longer depending on the level of prior training of educators and district leaders. For full implementation to be achieved, a minimum of 50% of staff need to be implementing the usable practice consistently and with fidelity. Additionally, all the implementation strategies have to be working individually and as a unit to maintain 50% of staff in consistent implementation.

Implementation Teams. The action plan template asks you to identify who is on the implementation team for each of the S.M.A.R.T. goals identified. These teams often shift based on roles and responsibilities within each district. It is important to identify the roles tasked with each step of the action planning process to both build individual accountability for the plan and to develop a district-wide institutional accountability to the continual engagement and completion of all the outlined outcome goals. Some important reminders: (1) Choose individuals you know will engage others, spread out the work, and see each step through to completion. (2) Be cognizant about the diversity of each team—teams should be made up of multiple social identities and roles. (3) Embed the responsibility of carrying out the strategic plan within outlined district roles and not just individuals—knowing that individuals come and go and district-based roles remain.

EXAMPLE TEAM:

If one of your S.M.A.R.T. goals is to review and revise the code of conduct, it will be critical to have a team consisting of individuals who created and uphold the code (e.g., district administrator, teachers, paraprofessionals, school leaders) as well as individuals most impacted by the code (e.g., students, family members).

Implementation Strategies. The "implementation drivers," or strategies, as we call them in the action plan, are the action steps that will be carried out to meet each of the outlined S.M.A.R.T. goals to inevitably meet the annual outcome goal. For example, an implementation team may need to "identify CR-SE research–based early literacy instructional practices" to support the academic improvement of the MTSS. The strategy could go on to say, "The implementation team will develop two full-day trainings on CR-SE research–based early literacy instructional practices." In the action plan, be clear about what implementation steps each S.M.A.R.T. goal requires and be as specific as possible about the action steps needed to get there.

Improvement Cycles. Plan-do-study-act (PDSA) cycles are used to test and build evidence that change is actually occurring. They are used for educators trained to plan for the implementation of the usable practice and to implement the practice based on the developed plan. As the implementation team moves through implementation strategies, there must be points of periodic review. Implementation is ideally processed through PDSA cycles to study what happened, including asking if the plan was implemented as intended; to discuss any challenges; and to analyze any measures of effectiveness that were used. The final part of this cycle (during the same meeting) focuses on identifying what went well and what didn't go well, and revising if need be.

As you make revisions in your plan, identify how often this implementation team will meet for PDSA improvement cycles and what data will be useful during cycles to further discuss the implementation of the overall usable practice. There are several helpful resources online that outline how teams can incrementally move through PDSA cycles within the outlined multiyear plan. In the action plan template we provided in Appendix D, it is important to identify when PDSA cycles will take place during the year as you move to accomplish each annual outcome goal. Table 4.40 provides a district example for each component of their Year 1 action plan.

Table 4.40. Year 1 Action Plan

Overall Outcome Goal Year 1:

By June 2024, the Tier 1 behavioral MTSS will be reviewed and revised.

S.M.A.R.T. GOALS	Implementation Phase	Implementation Team	Implementation Strategies	Start Date/ End Date	Improvement Cycles (PDSA)
By June 2024, review and revise the code of character, conduct and support (CCCS) to assess inclusive language and processes for racially, culturally, and linguistically marginalized students and families.	Initial implementation	Spring team chosen by superintendent, CR-SE/CCCS team, and inclusion of student/parent voice.	Review and revise the CCCS. Form a new team that combines members of the CR-SE team with the CCCS. Identify students and families of color who will be part of the CCCS review. Develop a schedule throughout the school day and/or evening so that students and parents can attend. The CoC/CR-SE team creates a survey to hear parents' perceptions/experiences with the code of conduct and include specific questions from 5th to 12th grade as they will be part of the development team.	April 2024–June 2024	On a periodic basis during school year 2024/2025, (i.e., August, November, February, and May) check for progress in the following areas: Code of conduct review and revisions of parent survey data collection and results.
By December 2024, review and revise the behavior referral process to assess inclusive language and processes responsive to racially, culturally, and linguistically marginalized students and families.		SSC team will review student behavior referral process.	Student behavior referral process to be reviewed by CCCS/CR-SE team to identify bias and ensure the form reflects a systemic format that aligns with the dashboard where data are entered. Revise behavior referral form based on findings.		Behavior referral form review and necessary revisions at bimonthly meeting.

(continued)

Table 4.40 (continued)

S.M.A.R.T. GOALS	Implementation Phase	Implementation Team	Implementation Strategies	Start Date/ End Date	Improvement Cycles (PDSA)
By June 2024, elementary social emotional learning (SEL) Building Committee will review and revise the Second Step[3] social-emotional learning curriculum (see glossary).	Installation	Elementary Building Committee; to include student voice, meetings will be during lunch or after school. Student voice will include selection of students through the student council.	Get New York University Culturally Responsive Checklist to review and compare to Second Step curriculum. Integrate an addendum to the Second Step curriculum that incorporates culturally responsive practices into the curriculum.	Summer 2024 June 2024	On a periodic basis during school year 2024/2025, the SEL committees will meet and check for progress. In the summer, the committee will begin with first curriculum units, then every other month elementary meetings to discuss how the process is going, what is going well, and what the challenges are to keep moving the work forward.

110

By June 2024, the leadership team and pupil personnel services will review use of restorative practices in the classroom to plan for ongoing support and implementation for teachers and staff.	Installation	Leadership team and PPS	Review use of restorative practices in classrooms by monitoring referrals and outcomes through SchoolTool and BryteBites data. Review the need for more training. Provide ongoing training and implementation support to teachers and staff. Develop a plan to continue to train new staff as they are hired. SSC and PPS will be trained in restorative practices. SSC and PPS will develop an assessment of effectiveness by comparing SchoolTool data. On a monthly basis, PPS will communicate with mental health teams, teachers, and teacher assistants to facilitate restorative practices with struggling students.	October 2024– June 2024	During PPS quarterly meetings, referrals and outcomes will be monitored through SchoolTool, and the use of restorative practices. Ongoing communication with leadership (through the Director of Pupil Support Services) and then with faculty will occur.

DIRECTIONS AS YOU MOVE THROUGH ACTION PLANNING

See Appendix D in the Chapter 4 appendices (https://www.tcpress.com /filebin/PDFs/9780807769447_app.pdf) for the blank template.

1. *Finalize your focus area(s)*—based on the evidence outlined in your root cause profile. Again, out of the root cause analysis, teams often end up with 2–4 focus areas. Any more can dilute the process and can be overwhelming, thus impacting future success. Ensure that focus areas are directly connected to the root cause analysis.
2. *Develop your culturally responsive usable practice*—based on your focus area (each focus area has a usable practice). Write the statement that will be the dominant practice throughout the multiyear plan. Use culturally responsive language similar to what you see identified in the action plan example. Here is another example of a culturally responsive usable practice for a family engagement focus area:
    Identify, develop, and implement a sustainable system for family and community engagement that ensures representation of racially, culturally, and linguistically marginalized families in order to build effective ongoing communication between community members and the school district staff.
3. *Create outcome goals for at least years 1, 2, and 3* (or up to 5 years).
4. Start with year 1 and break down the annual outcome goal into the S.M.A.R.T. goals that will lead to successful implementation.
5. *Move through the rest of the template,* identifying the implementation phase, implementation team, implementation strategies, timeline, and a plan for any embedded improvement cycles.
6. *Complete the same process for years 2 and 3.*

ACTION PLANNING TIP

Perfection is never achieved. It is more important to move through each step as best as possible rather than getting stuck trying to negotiate every single potential barrier. Sometimes the barrier is ourselves. We often witness teams living in "structural tensions," naming all the reasons a goal can't be achieved and avoiding accountability for potential change. Move with courage and know that this process is iterative and is intended to be revised as teams continue to meet.

AVOIDING DETOURS: DISTRICT SUCCESSES AND CHALLENGES

While we have explained the practical application with a district to move through the critical root cause processes, we want to take this time to highlight important successes and challenges with various districts as they engaged through the process. We offer these as guideposts that include best practices as well as pitfalls and detours to avoid.

Good Data Sources

When we send our data request to our partnering districts, we tend to encounter one of two responses: (1) districts that have a robust data system, easily able to pull out data and fulfill our request, or (2) districts with a poor data system where it immediately becomes challenging to find data. Data are either unavailable or not collected, or multiple data systems are being used that do not communicate with one another. Another challenge is not having district staff who know how to locate the data or utilize the data systems. Districts need designated personnel who are familiar with the storage, coding, and purpose and correct use of data. For both the root cause analysis process and the ongoing work, it is critical for districts to analyze disaggregated student outcomes, identify which students are disproportionately impacted, and continuously use data to take action.

Acknowledging the Data and Taking Action

The detour of denying and explaining data away leads to not taking action to address disproportionality (Carter et al., 2017). When districts begin examining their data, we have witnessed educators at times denying and explaining away the data. This often includes not believing that it's their data, which leads to recalculating the data while in training sessions. Further, in mostly white districts, when districts have lower enrollment of students of color, they tend to minimize the data and the experiences that students of color are having. We have heard educators say, "It's only five Black students; is that significant?"

Superintendent Framing and Communication

As the leader of the district, the superintendent's framing around the importance of equity and CR-SE work is critical. In districts where the superintendent has messaged the work on an ongoing basis, the district has continued to make progress. This communication allows various stakeholders to have a shared language and be part of the work. Further, it offers the conditions for buying into the work and developing a collaborative culture (Fullan & Quinn, 2016). For instance, one of the superintendents in a district in which we partnered came out on the first day of training and identified the student community who had been most impacted by disproportionality and acknowledged the impact of race and racism on the schooling community. Their messaging and modeling during the first root cause training session set the tone and expectations for the remaining sessions and their next steps. During the sessions, their communication continued to be constant, and the superintendent pushed the team to use shared language to further push team members who had bought into the work as well as colleagues who were uncertain.

Preparedness to Engage Work

For districts that have not yet had conversations about the ways that race and racism impacts students of color and intersecting marginalized identities, it is important that they engage in preparatory book study. (See Appendix E in the Chapter 4 appendices [https://www.tcpress.com/filebin/PDFs/9780807769447_app.pdf] for a resource list.) For instance, some of the educators in a partnering district struggled in Session 1 to consider that race was shaping the experiences and outcomes for students of color. We modified the root cause training sessions to integrate a study of the book *White Fragility* (DiAngelo, 2018) with a mostly white staff. Engaging in this process allowed the mostly white team to engage in an individual and institutional reflective space as they examined their student outcome data, their policies, and their practices. Most critically, it allowed them to engage in the beliefs that were leading to their disparities. When districts fail to prepare ahead, we witness detours in stakeholders not identifying which students and families are mostly impacted, denying the data, and derailing the work during training sessions.

Board Member Involvement

Board member involvement is essential to move the work forward. We have found that when board members are a part of the work, they are able to leverage their learnings from the root cause process to develop common language, to take a deeper dive on how board policies are impacting students and families, and to message the work to other board members and nonparticipating stakeholders. Having norms becomes even more important when board members are a part of the process—in particular, the norm of maintaining a confidential space. When we frame confidentiality, we reinforce that if you hold positional power—which includes board members and building/district leaders—personal experiences that team members share remain in the sessions, and stress the impact it has on a team when confidentiality is not held.

Knowledgeable Team Members

In Chapter 3, we describe who needs to be part of the root cause team. The selected team members must have knowledge of the policies, practices, and procedures that exist in the district and how they are implemented in the district and individual schools. For instance, having a district staff member who has experience in MTSS alongside multiple teachers and pupil support services personnel creates the condition in which the district staff can offer the purpose, available supports, and MTSS intended implementation, while teachers and staff can share its use in schools. Further, having parents/caregivers as part of the root cause team offers team members of the district insight on how policies, practices, and procedures are directly impacting families and their children.

CONCLUSION

As you have moved through a district example for you to practice with, we leave you with next steps for completing your district's root cause analysis. In starting the root cause analysis process, it is important to keep in mind that effective root cause processes seek to unearth the inequities that exist in a given community and to give voice to historically and currently marginalized students and families. When districts can acknowledge and unapologetically take action on which students and families are impacted the most, equity is then possible. That means recognizing the impact that systems of whiteness, racism, and oppression have on historically and currently marginalized students, families, and communities. When districts and schools bypass this, it leads to maintaining schooling environments that continue to exclude and harm the same children (Gorski, 2019).

CRITICAL QUESTIONS

1) How have you prepared for the root cause analysis in your district?
2) What will your district have to do to avoid barriers and detours to effective implementation?
3) What is your plan to message the work?

How Can Districts and Schools Leverage Student Voice in Addressing Disproportionality?

> The more students work at storing the deposits entrusted to them, the less they develop the critical consciousness which would result from their intervention in the world as transformers of that world.
>
> —Paulo Freire (Freire & Macedo, 1970)

One key principle within culturally responsive and sustaining education is the centering of youth voice. Today's students are well aware of disparities within schooling and deserve the platform to discuss and address those disparities collectively. Critical educator Paulo Freire believed that one's education should serve to question the world, read the world, and read oneself and their positionality.[1] One way to read the world in relation to one's self is through participatory action research (PAR), which is rooted in Freire's concept of *conscientizãcao,* or critical consciousness (Lykes & Mallona, 2008). Only when those most marginalized reclaim power, and have control and decision-making power, can radical change happen.

This chapter will provide a framework, process, and tools that help districts and schools to build student voice to address disproportionality. This work stems from the formation of the first-ever youth arm of the Center for Disproportionality (CfD), which birthed the Youth Center for Disproportionality (YCfD). The group represented 15 different schools across a large northeastern city that we refer to as Lightpoint. YCfD set out to explore disproportionality in hopes of advocating for more equitable schooling conditions. Through participatory action research, YCfD critically examined the structural inequities of their education system in hopes of advancing schooling to be more humanizing for all students. Ultimately, this meant that students advocated to feel respected, affirmed, welcomed, and validated in schools through recommended policies such as culturally responsive curriculum and restorative justice. YCfD's mission was to advance equity by disrupting, dismantling, and eradicating disproportionality by building the capacity of educators to implement culturally responsive and sustainable equity-based systems that meet the needs of every student.

Please note that this chapter is not a step-by-step instruction manual on implementing youth voice and equitable youth adult partnerships within schools and districts. Instead, this chapter provides a set of guidelines and suggestions. We do not believe in a "one-size-fits-all" solution and are acutely aware that schools and districts have their own unique characteristics. This work should ultimately center one's own contexts, capacities, and, most of all, the youth toward addressing disproportionality. With investment, commitment, hard work, and dedication, along with capacity-building and systemic reform, important change will follow. This chapter provides an example and inspiration for "doing the work" that is necessary for *every* child to meet their potential.

(RE)DEFINING DISPROPORTIONALITY

As part of our process and political education, YCfD redefined the term "disproportionality." As a result of our historical political exploration of disproportionality, our group felt it necessary to revise the U.S. Department of Education's definition of disproportionality, as it was insufficient to its actual meaning. The students worked together to chart the root causes and outcomes of disproportionality. After several attempts to get it "right," YCfD defined disproportionality as *"the outcome of institutionalized racism and bias that result in discriminatory beliefs, policies, and practices, which negatively affect historically marginalized groups in contrast to privileged groups."* A strong and trustworthy partnership between youth and adults, along with political education, were foundational and ongoing parts of this process.

SOLIDIFYING SUSTAINING YOUTH-ADULT PARTNERSHIPS

The first step is to establish a strong and sustaining youth-adult partnership. Youth remain at the center of this work, providing the necessary guidance, leadership, and knowledge in helping adults understand their experiences so that adults can fully support students. Youth, and particularly youth from historically marginalized backgrounds, have an understanding of educational problems not only at an interpersonal level, but also as shaped by systemic and structural forces (Renick et al., 2021). However, student opinions are often overlooked or tokenized in schools that largely function as sites of discipline and control, despite perpetuating values of democracy (Oto, 2023). Therefore, youth and adult partnerships in dismantling disproportionality must combat *adultism*, the notion that adults are consistently mature and rational, whereas youth are not (LeFrançois, 2014), and instead allow students to take the lead in their own liberatory pursuit.

What Does a Youth-Adult Partnership Look Like?

A productive youth-adult partnership is possible when the adult supports youth and youth voice. Often, equality is viewed as the end goal of a youth-adult partnership; however, equality simply does not go far enough to redress power issues. When student voice is second to those of adults, the decision-making power of youth is quickly diminished and their inclusion in these spaces becomes performative, which emphasizes the "dramatic form of asymmetry between youth and adults" (Mitra, 2009, p. 409). To support youth voice, adults should recognize that students are the highest authority on their own experiences and needs and therefore youth and adults cannot have equal roles in creating change. This view of youth-adult partnerships pushes past Hart's "Ladder of Young People's Participation" (Figure 5.1) toward what we call a "Youth-Driven Ladder

Figure 5.1. Hart's Ladder of Young People's Participation

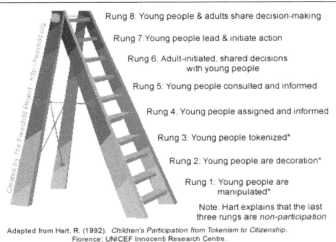

Rung 8: Young people & adults share decision-making

Rung 7: Young people lead & initiate action

Rung 6: Adult-initiated, shared decisions with young people

Rung 5: Young people consulted and informed

Rung 4: Young people assigned and informed

Rung 3: Young people tokenized*

Rung 2: Young people are decoration*

Rung 1: Young people are manipulated*

Note: Hart explains that the last three rungs are *non-participation*

Adapted from Hart, R. (1992). *Children's Participation from Tokenism to Citizenship*. Florence: UNICEF Innocenti Research Centre.

Figure 5.2. Youth-Driven Ladder of Participation

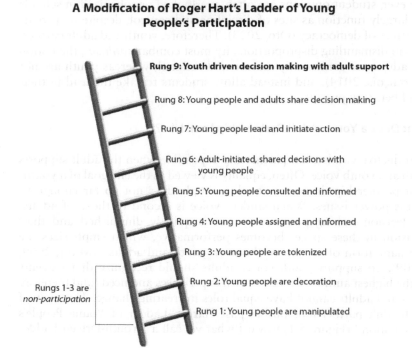

A Modification of Roger Hart's Ladder of Young People's Participation

Rung 9: Youth driven decision making with adult support

Rung 8: Young people and adults share decision making

Rung 7: Young people lead and initiate action

Rung 6: Adult-initiated, shared decisions with young people

Rung 5: Young people consulted and informed

Rung 4: Young people assigned and informed

Rung 3: Young people are tokenized

Rung 2: Young people are decoration

Rungs 1-3 are *non-participation*

Rung 1: Young people are manipulated

Adapted and modified from Hart, R. (1992). *Children's Participation from Tokenism to Citizenship.* Florence: UNICEF Innocenti Research Centre.

of Participation" (Figure 5.2). We propose a 9th rung of "equitable part-nerships" where youth drive decision-making and adults support their efforts to enact change to advance educational justice. This means that the adult's role is to fully support the youth, as youth initiate decision-making and surface issues of concern.

ESTABLISHING THE PARTNERSHIP

To establish the partnership, a school or district representative must make a commitment to address educational inequity. This adult representative, or **adult partner**, is ideally a separate paid position or structured within an existing job description. The adult partner coordinates logistics of the group to move the work along. Ideal characteristics of the supporting adult include (but are not limited to):

- A district representative or school representative (depending on the scope of the project).
- Reliable, trustworthy, and invested in equity.
  - » The adult (or team of adults) is/are deeply invested in equity—meaning they have a sense of what disproportionality is and its root causes. Ideally, they were a member of the district's root cause team (see Chapter 3), if this district participated in a root cause analysis. They are not afraid to address issues such as race and racism and other issues of power and privilege. They are willing to learn and grow with the immediate group and surrounding colleagues.
  - » The adult must also be willing to challenge and work with their colleagues and superiors to stand in solidarity with youth toward the end goal of equitable schooling structures.
  - » The adult has done their personal work around identity, race, power, and privilege. The adult continues this internal interrogation throughout their work with youth.
- Presents follow-through.
  - » Helps work with youth to coordinate meetings and other events.
  - » Has access to resources such as food and space.
  - » Holds other adults—both those intimately involved in the project and those who are not—accountable for filling their roles and fulfilling promises so that youth can adequately do their work.
- Builds bridges between youth and education stakeholders.
- Has a positive reputation among students for connecting with youth and being responsive to youth, and is a recognized advocate of students from historically marginalized communities.
- Handles logistics such as parent permission forms and communication with schools.
- Is familiar with the "lay of the land."
  - » This person understands the structure of the school and district and the politics of the district, and knows the right people to get things done.
- Grounds their trust in youth by stepping back and encourages youth leadership in the immediate group and throughout classrooms and other educational spaces.

In some cases, the group may want to identify a neutral space for meeting, such as a local library, community center, or university facilities. This way, students can begin the conversation safely away from school and district leadership. In a neutral territory, students can take the lead on issues without fear of infiltration and negative opinions from unsupportive school adults. Overall, the characteristics listed above are consistent with what CfD encourages for district readiness and engagement.

Recruitment of Students

Ideally, all students would take a role in this work. Realistically, however, not all students will join enthusiastically, due to lack of interest, lack of trust, or other time constraints. Therefore, we do not encourage this as mandatory for students. There should be multiple pathways for students to participate given their capacity and interest. Some students may only assist at certain parts of the process, such as assistance with data collection or analysis. Others may be more invested in the political education portion. Further, youth attrition is normal, but that should not reduce momentum. With that said, *a core group of committed students is the key to getting things done.*

Students recruited to this group should ideally be representative of the student body in regard to race, socioeconomic status, gender, sexuality, academic status, grade level, leadership involvement, school engagement, and disciplinary status. Students enter school with different sets of circumstances and identities that determine their experience within the learning environment. Black students experience school differently than white students, than Asian students, Latinx students, and Indigenous students, and so forth. As highlighted in previous chapters, Black students in particular experience disproportionate discipline and enrollment into remedial courses (Morris, 2016; U.S. Government Accountability Office, 2018). Furthermore, some students may have special needs or vary in gender expression; therefore, it's important to have representation. Vulnerable students, or students from historically marginalized backgrounds, tend to be more comfortable sharing their truths with other students (rather than authority figures) because they may share similar experiences and will not fear punishment. Therefore, students are more likely to have access to the voices of their peers than adults.

That being said, the group must center the voices of students who are most marginalized even if they are in the minority (Malone et al., 2023). Students who have the most difficult time with school are needed voices, as white or privileged students cannot fully grasp the experiences of ostracized groups. It is important for white students to understand whiteness, how it functions, and to explicitly decenter whiteness in conversations (DiAngelo,

2018). For instance, in a predominately white school, it is necessary for Black and Brown voices to be heard and supported even if they are a smaller percentage. We believe that uplifting marginalized students will provide a more equitable and humanizing experience for all students (Ginwright, 2015). It is necessary that in this partnership, Black and Brown and other vulnerable students are not silenced.

Youth Role. Youth enter this partnership with knowledge, experiences, and the ability to communicate with other students in a way that adults cannot. For instance, students are uniquely affected by school policies and practices such as teacher-student relationships and curriculum and instruction. Student experiences vary in terms of how they might see themselves reflected in learning materials and/or their teachers, which affects their level of engagement and sense of belonging (Paris & Alim, 2017). Further, youth can often gauge the effects of school culture better than an administrative assessment tool because of their embodied knowledge of their school experience. For example, one of our students, Jessica, who is one of the few Black students at her school, explained to us and her administration the discomfort and discrimination she experienced with her school's disciplinary policy on durags and bonnets (Black haircare accessories). Because the school's policies were rooted in whiteness, Black students who refused to assimilate into "professional" (read, white middle-class norms) were punished. Jessica and her peers' insights were invaluable in raising those points to reform school culture to support Black students and all students at her campus.

Therefore, youth have a critical role in this partnership. Some roles and responsibilities include:

- Creating the mission, vision, and values of the organization
- Planning or co-planning meeting sessions and topics
- Facilitating or co-facilitating planning and general meetings
- Hosting meetings with school leadership to turnkey information
- Disseminating information to youth beyond the group
- Determining the trajectory, goals, and activities of the team

Adult Role. Adults enter this partnership with years of experience, institutional knowledge, and an investment in equity. Again, the idea is for adults to *support* students and lead this work toward transformational change at an institutional level. Adult roles and responsibilities include but are not limited to:

- Providing resources and informing students of systemic racism and oppression in schools (policies, budgeting, politics) or other barriers so that they can tackle them together

- Offering students literature and history related to the current educational context
- Providing students with necessary contact information for key administrators and decision-makers who are gatekeepers for critical change
- Providing access to data (e.g., achievement data, discipline data, student interviews)
- Serving as a liaison between students and their adult counterparts
- Pushing policy change at the school and district levels

Overall, adults should use their power to support and inform youth choices, not overpower them.

In order to have a sustaining and solid youth-adult partnership, it is important for everyone to understand their roles. Adults must listen to youth and let their experiences guide the work. Further, adults must have an understanding of inequity and be able to offer insight of their knowledge on the sociohistorical political landscape of schooling to deepen conversations and make transformative change to better the schooling experiences of youth.

Now that we have laid out the expectations of a sustaining equitable youth-adult partnership, we move to a common understanding of a respectful and nurturing space when youth and adults come together to do educational equity work. We adapt the concept of "contact zone" to guide us toward establishing a generative youth-adult space during working meetings.

ESTABLISHING A CONTACT ZONE

Youth voice sessions (held in partnership with adults) consist of a systematic anti-racist, progressive curriculum that sparks a sociopolitical-historical understanding of current issues through data, literature, and deeply engaged dialogue. Before these lessons and conversations take place, it is necessary to create a generative space.

Creating a Contact Zone

Before diving into the intense work of pulling apart the threads of disproportionality, it is necessary to form a safe, supportive, trustworthy, and loving environment to do this work. Equity work requires a conducive environment, which is often referred to as a "safe space" or even a "brave space," where students are meant to feel emotionally and physically safe and supported despite differences. Unfortunately, too often, these "safe" spaces silence students from speaking their truths for fear of breaking up "peace" within a space while their social identities risk erasure and marginalization. Equity work is not necessarily "safe" (particularly for our youth). Students risk invoking the anger of teachers and administrators who have control over their academic trajectory and their security within the school community. The youth take on this risk while reliving traumas as they unpack their experiences. A "brave" space often encourages participants to speak out about difficult topics but does not take power differences of social identities into account. For instance, a queer Black student may take the risk of disrupting white heteronormative ideologies, which might make themselves vulnerable to the group's dominant beliefs. Instead, a contact zone is an intentional space of intergenerational, multiracial, and diverse participants who engage on politicized topics. In a contact zone, dynamics of power and oppression are recognized, and those with more privilege are called in to ally with those who have marginalized identities. In this section, we flesh out what a contact zone is and how we formed it.

Forming a Contact Zone

We draw on Maria Torre's concept of a "contact zone" to form a safe and generative space for our equity work. Torre notes that "by framing our PAR collective as a contact zone, we create a politically and intellectually charged space where very differently positioned youth and adults are able to experience and analyze power inequities, together" (2008, p. 24). Our space was indeed *politically* and *intellectually* charged given our different identities, not just racially and socioeconomically, but due to age, experience, and other factors. These "invisible" factors were very much a part of our space. We find this contact zone critical. As Torre wrote,

> Privileged youth who otherwise might opt out of such work (as it potentially challenges a system which benefits them) ally with historically marginalized youth, who also might not have joined the research collective (as they have learned well that change is slow and promises are rarely kept). As a collective, we have used our differences (rather than ignoring them) to further thinking, research, writing and speaking on educational equity and change. (2008, p. 24)

Before the group is critical of systems and challenges in our institutions, the individuals have to be critical of themselves. Members must challenge themselves to think about their own biases and how they came to understand the world around them. Similar to the work required of our adult educators, youth with white privilege, male privilege, hetero-sexual privilege, and other privileges have to interrogate their positional-ity and be co-conspirators[2] for the more vulnerable identities in the room. In YCfD, we aimed to build solidarity before pushing for larger scale edu-cational equity reform. This means (as Torre put it):

- Connecting "personal struggles" with historic struggles for justice
- Converting individual experiences of pain and oppression into structural analyses and demands for justice
- Interrogating the unfairness of privilege
- Linking activist research to youth organizing movements for social justice

The contact zone gives students ample opportunities to share personal experiences. These share-outs were important in building connection and community, but also helped us understand a larger context by situating personal experiences within a historical and political pursuit for equity.

Learning About Each Other

Because of our differences, YCfD intentionally set up an environment where we came to know and trust one another. In each meeting, we took time to build community in order to establish an environment rooted in respect and love. View Table 5.1 for suggestions on establishing com-munity norms and Table 5.2 for community-building. Just as community norms are established for adult participants (as outlined in Chapter 1), we model that within our youth-centered work.

Through community-building and establishing norms, we fostered a positive rapport with one another, where we had the support struc-ture in place for people to disagree with one another and learn from one another's perspectives. Students remarked during our meetings that they were glad to learn about one another's different experiences, es-pecially given that their own school communities are like a "bubble" considering the racial and class segregation of the city's schools. YCfD aligned with Torre's description of a contact zone as "a messy social space where differently situated people 'meet, clash, and grapple with each other' across their varying relationships to power" (Pratt [1991] quoted in Torre, 2008, p. 4).

By viewing ourselves as a "contact zone," we learned much from one another. Members of YCfD felt safe to show up as who they were, inter-rogating themselves in order to build loving and meaningful relationships with other members. It was necessary to build a strong community and

Table 5.1. Establish Community Norms

Establish community norms (a set of practices rooted in a sense of shared values and beliefs that foster respect and love for one another). The norms should be co-created. Below are examples of community norms we charted at one of our first meetings:

- Have one mic.
- One person speaks while everyone else listens.
- Step up, step back.
- If you are talking and taking too much space more than others, step back. If you are silent most of the time, step up.
- Know and check your power/privilege.
- Those with privilege reflect on how their experiences are impacted by societal advantages such as white privilege, heteronormativity, and patriarchy.
- Everyone plays a role.
- There must be shared leadership and responsibility for everyone involved.
- Use "I" statements.
- A style of communication that centers the feelings and beliefs of the speaker, rather than generalizations and/or the thoughts that the speaker attributes to the listeners.
- Challenge others but seek understanding, not an argument.

Table 5.2. Examples of Community-Building in a Contact Zone

We learned one another's names, origin, and the meanings of our names	Sat in a circle as much as possible to interrupt hierarchy
Discussed our experiences in our respective schools	Allowed members to participate in a variety of ways, such as verbal, written, or artistic expression
Opportunities to share about one another's identities	Small-group conversations

foundation for us to then take a deep dive into understanding and addressing disproportionality.

As one of our youth participants, Jayla, remarked:

This group did not just give me a sense of home. Since everyone was close and shared similar ideas on different topics, and respectfully disagreed with each other. But the sense of belonging, to know there are teenagers with similar mindsets. It is so easy to feel misunderstood in a school where you are the only one that sees the injustice and wants to do something about it but do not have the proper support system to do so. But this group finally gave me a haven where everyone sees the unjust, wants to make a difference, and an amazing support system.—Jayla, YCfD, Cohort 2

POLITICAL EDUCATION

Before taking action to address disproportionality (such as shifting policies and practices) with adult allies and the greater community, it is necessary to invest the time to learn about current issues and their deep historical root causes. Of course, education is never neutral (cf Henry Giroux); what educators teach in school are inherently political decisions. Too often, an exploration of power and privilege is left out of the classroom. Given that schooling outcomes are raced and classed, it was necessary for YCfD to first implement an unapologetic anti-racist, critical, and humanizing curriculum. Together, we addressed a broad range of issues surrounding education and its sociopolitical historical context. Further, in the planning stages, topics were driven by youth, with support of a well-informed and well-trained adult on topics of equity and justice.

In our first few sessions, we defined the terms *equality*, *equity*, *fairness*, *opportunity*, and *access* as related to the political context of the education system. We also defined the terms *race*, *class*, *culture*, and *ethnicity* and how these terms differ and intersect (for key terms and definitions, see the Chapter 5 appendices, Appendix A, https://www.tcpress.com/filebin/PDFs/9780807769447_app.pdf). We offer these interactive tables to model our process and so that you can apply them to your school context as well.

In our discussions we veered away from color-evasive language and ideologies, as they are detrimental to students of color and uphold whiteness. Facilitators used several real-world examples and current events to help illuminate the root causes of disproportionality. These examples often spurred rich dialogue, where students added their own experiences that helped deepen understandings. The relevant topics in the Chapter 5 appendices, Appendix B (https://www.tcpress.com/filebin/PDFs/9780807769447_app.pdf), were identified by youth, and it is important to add your own that is germane to your context.

THE YPAR PROJECT

The next step in the process was the youth participatory action research (YPAR) project to deepen an understanding of disproportionality and its outcomes in the context of students' own local schools. The political education and curriculum outlined earlier was a necessary step before taking on the YPAR project because it helped set the context for the project by deepening knowledge on disproportionality. After extensive political education and deep discussions, the YPAR project gave us the space and opportunity to further understand the lived experience of how students were impacted by disproportionality in their everyday realities.

Why Youth Participatory Action Research?

YCfD adopted a youth participatory action research (YPAR) framework. YPAR is an epistemology that engages collective action of a group where academics and participants democratically engage in research design, methods, and analyses (Torre, 2009). YPAR is rooted in Freire's critical praxis and stems from the principles of critical pedagogy of examining power and positionality. In YPAR, students take the lead in their own liberation and interrogate their positionality within dominant structures. Cammarota and Fine (2008) note that in utilizing YPAR, "education is something students do—instead of being done to them—to address the injustices that limit possibilities for them, their families, and communities" (p. 10). Given that our education largely excludes youth from the decision-making process despite their knowledge of their own needs, YPAR has the potential to radically transform schooling in advancing equity. Addressing disproportionality and the oppressive structures that birthed these inequitable outcomes cannot be properly addressed without participation from those who are most disenfranchised—our Black, Brown, and vulnerable youth.

Executing a YPAR Project

There is no magic formula for executing a perfect YPAR project. It is often a messy, organic process. PAR is conducted in many different ways. Ultimately, the project will bend and reflect a group's particular context and capacity. In this section, we outline suggestions of the typical steps of a YPAR project and what worked for us. Typically, a PAR project includes the following steps:

1. Facilitating/conducting political education
2. Identifying a problem
3. Collecting preliminary data (learning about the context of local settings)
   a. Quantitative data collection
   b. Qualitative (observation) data collection
4. Posing a question
5. Identifying tools needed to answer the question
6. Collecting data
7. Performing collective analysis of the data
8. Drawing conclusions (findings)

Before getting started, it's helpful to have an outline of what your goals are. Review the Chapter 5 appendices, Appendix C (https://www.tcpress.com/filebin/PDFs/9780807769447_app.pdf), for a sample timeline. Keep in mind that deadlines and goals may be adjusted accordingly. Appendix D in the Chapter 5 appendices provides a template for you to create your own YPAR project timeline.

Preliminary Data Collection (Learning About the Context of Local Settings)

Early in the research process, YCfD engaged in capturing the context of Lightpoint's educational landscape. As you can see from the timeline, we spent the first 2 months gathering contextual data to give us more information about the culture of our schools. In this process we looked at (a) quantitative data, and (b) qualitative (observation) data.

Quantitative Data Collection. We wanted to understand the social context and "hard data," or numbers of students who were suspended, disaggregated by race, and other identifying factors. For us to further our knowledge on disproportionality, we reviewed quantitative achievement and behavioral data, disaggregated by race. We looked at National Public School Achievement, the National Assessment of Education Progress (NAEP), for reading and math in the 4th- and 8th-grade test scores. Furthermore, we reviewed state data controlling for poverty. For this data analysis, we conducted a gallery walk, reviewing the data displayed on visual charts and graphs, and then taped them around the room. CfD members took their time reviewing the data points that were posted around the room. During the gallery walk, we wrote comments on sticky notes about what surprised us or stood out to us about the data.

In another session, we looked at Lightpoint's district behavioral data. The students broke into groups and reviewed data from the city's various neighborhoods that their respective school was a part of. In order to review those data, students learned about interpreting the *risk index* and *relative risk ratio* (see Chapter 3). Risk index identifies at what rate, or percentage of risk, students of a racial/ethnic group have in a particular outcome. Relative risk ratio are comparisons of the risks of a particular outcome of one group to the risk of the remaining group(s) experiencing the same outcome. This is the same process that the adults engaged in the CfD root cause sessions.

Reviewing and analyzing the quantitative data was not as challenging as the adult facilitators anticipated for students—they talked with ease about trends they found in the data. The youth even brought up limitations of the data, asking questions such as "What about Muslim students? Or refugees? Or LGBTQ+ students? Or Black students who are Latinx and vice versa?" Students quickly humanized the data, meaning that they brought the quantitative data to life by relaying their own experiences and connections to the disparities they saw in the data, and began to relate it to what they observed in their own schools.

Qualitative (Observation) Data Collection. To complement our quantitative data collection, YCfD participants set out to explore the following question: *What policies and practices are implemented at your school that reinforce disproportionality?* The task for students was to think about their respective schools as researchers. Students were to look at their code of conduct, classroom rules and policies, or any observed inconsistencies in discipline practices between different students in regard to race or other identifying factors. The following are tools that helped YCfD with this process:

YCfD Walkthrough Observation Protocol. This tool (Chapter 5 appendices, Appendix E, https://www.tcpress.com/filebin/PDFs/978080 7769447_app.pdf) helps determine *school culture* through school walkthroughs and observations. Please feel free to adjust this tool to fit your own school climate, reflecting your school culture, appropriate mannerisms, and other school-specific routines and norms. The tool is intended for youth and adults to use together to determine school culture and the student experience. With this tool, schools can begin critical conversations with youth and adult stakeholders about what contributes to/and or disrupts an equitable school environment. The hope is that the conversations will lead to action and necessary policy changes.

After using these tools, youth shared their observations of noticeable outcomes of disproportionality, such as the lack of racial diversity among classmates and teachers, or the presence of metal detectors and high number of security guards in predominantly Black and Brown schools.

Below are examples of findings for this research activity. Each student response is from a different school:

> We are majority Black and Latino; however, suspension rate is extremely high. In addition to the zero tolerance policy, our students are not being reasoned with. Instead they are being punished more harshly than what they should be. Only approximately 10 of 98 students are taking AP Calc (our only AP class). We also only have two Honors classes, one being when you are already a senior.

> In a school with a majority white staff, most students feel misrepresented and misunderstood. Usually this is due to the teachers not taking into account students' struggles (regarding race, family, or financial instability, etc.).

> Demographic is majority white and Asian; thus students who are unequally represented feel isolated and even attacked sometimes. Our staff and teachers are majority white as well.

Not all responses were negative—another high school noted positive practices such as restorative circles and welcoming staff.

Although we considered this step in the YPAR process preliminary research, these are important data, and depending on how much time you have, you can expand the data collection. For instance, although we ran out of time, students could have even gone back to collect more information about how their schools function in regard to disproportionality. Despite our lack of time, this was an important process in prompting students to think about how disproportionality plays out in their school through their lens.

1. Pose a question.

After gathering an abundance of information on the context and culture of our individual schools, students were ready to delve even deeper into exploring disproportionality. They wanted to talk to their peers and understand how they experienced disproportionality. YCfD posed as their main research question, *How do youth who attend Lightpoint schools experience disproportionality?* After the walkthroughs and viewing the quantitative data on disproportionality, we now wanted to focus our efforts on collecting qualitative data that centered on youth and school adult perspectives regarding their embodied school experiences.

2. Identify what tools are needed to answer the question.

Our tools shifted a bit from year to year. However, YCfD was consistent in using qualitative methods (human-centered research) to fully understand the human experience under the guise of disproportionality. We decided to make and distribute an open-ended survey as the tool to help us answer our question. You may also decide to do focus groups or individual interviews, depending on the capacity of your group and context. The open-ended survey (described below) worked for us.

Qualitative Data Collection Survey. Each year a survey was distributed to understand the embodied school experience of young people (and in year 2, adults as well). Participants were given the option to respond through images (drawing a picture) or through written response to the prompt to gather a wider range of expression to make meaning of their experiences. View Chapter 5 appendices, Appendix F (https://www.tcpress .com/filebin/PDFs/9780807769447_app.pdf), to see the open-ended student survey that YCfD distributed.

Before launching our data collection, during one of our YCfD meetings we piloted the activity with our internal group. Everyone completed the activity and talked through their drawings. From there, the students were directed to conduct these same surveys with their classmates. Piloting the survey within the group helped youth understand the process of completing the survey and fielding questions from participants.

Data Collection (distributing the surveys). Students administered the survey in their respective school with support from the principal and staff liaison. Some schools were resistant, but most students found ways to distribute the survey to their peers and school adults.

To that end, the adult relationship becomes invaluable when youth are met with resistance from their school administration. Adult partners can support students in navigating these hurdles in order to facilitate the data collection. When youth have trouble distributing surveys or other information, adult partners can intervene by leveraging their power to help with the process. We understand that some teachers may also be vulnerable to pushback from school leadership, yet we encourage teachers to use their privilege when they can and build a greater collective of educators to support youth. Data collection is crucial to illuminating a problem and understanding the student experience. It is an opportunity for learning and building a stronger school community.

After conducting the qualitative survey with participants, the group came back together to reflect on our data collection process *before* analyzing the data. The YCfD youth researchers who were successful with the survey were able to request class time from their teacher for their fellow students to participate. Other YCfD students handed out the survey to their peers during lunch or their free time. YCfD members reported that some of their peers were interested and eager to take the survey, noting that they rarely have the opportunity to discuss this topic. Other YCfD members said that their classmates felt uncomfortable with it or that they weren't interested in taking it because "they didn't have Black and Brown kids at their schools."

For us, in the end, students collected over 100 surveys from their peers. Others collected a classroom size of surveys. For year 2, we collected nearly 500 surveys total. We had a large task ahead of analyzing the data. The following are tools that helped us make meaning of our completed surveys.

Collective Data Analysis. After the data collection comes the tedious and important task of analyzing the data. During this process we made sense of the data through a systematic and iterative process to draw conclusions. This process takes several weeks, as it is necessary to be thorough when establishing themes, outliers, and other interesting data points.

- **Data Dive.** The Data Dive worksheet and activity were useful in helping us pick apart surveys and help us unpack the data. In our case, we separated the surveys into boroughs,[3] and then within the five boroughs, we divided youth and adult surveys by race and gender. We provide a copy of our Data Dive worksheet in

  the Chapter 5 appendices, Appendix G (https://www.tcpress.com
  /filebin/PDFs/9780807769447_app.pdf).

- **Data Dive, Part 2.** The second round of our qualitative data
  analysis consisted of a grounded analysis, where we carefully
  looked at surveys and identified what themes we found. We
  discussed what was interesting about the images, what words
  or phrases stood out to us in the written explanations, and
  what was similar or different across various categories such
  as race, gender, school, or borough. We repeated this activity
  roughly three times to help us draw more conclusive results.
  You can view our Data Dive Part 2 worksheet in the Chapter 5
  appendices, Appendix H (https://www.tcpress.com/filebin/PDFs
  /9780807769447_app.pdf).

For our collective analysis, we used grounded theory (Glaser & Strauss,
1968), meaning that we applied inductive analysis to our data to group
emerging themes and from there generated theory. Together, we split up
the surveys into different piles. Then the whole group split up into smaller
groups of 4–5 people. YCfD adults and youth made up the groups. We
each took a pile and, together, read through the surveys. We began to
categorize responses that were similar to create themes. We highlighted
significant quotes from the surveys on sticky notes that we would share
later with the group for feedback. Next, in our groups we began to talk
about what we were noticing in the data. Lastly, each group decided on
themes identified from their specific pile. From there, we put our findings
on a large poster-sized sticky note. This was an iterative process, and we
completed several rounds to get many eyes and ideas on the different sets
of data before drawing conclusions.

  Each group put on the wall the poster that compiled their themes
and what they found complicated or interesting about the data, as well
as significant quotes they chose from the student responses. When all the
posters were up, we did a gallery walk to look at each poster. We looked
for differences and connections across posters to form themes. When the
gallery walk was over, students shared their own poster, and then other
students shared what themes and outliers they noticed.

  The 500+ responses we collected offered deeply personal reflections
on disproportionality; students drew images of themselves behind pris-
on bars, of their classmates yelling slurs, of discrimination from their
teachers, and so forth. They wrote about their ideal school—a school
that supported them, a school where they saw themselves in the teachers
and curriculum, a school that truly listened to their voices. The surveys
brought the lived experiences of students into our study of disproportionality, adding depth to our work. Furthermore, the process of bringing the

surveys into schools and classrooms validated students' experiences of disproportionality and disrupted the silence that had long accompanied them. Students who responded to the surveys were empowered to take ownership of their experiences, acknowledge any injustices they may have faced, and imagine what their ideal school could be. The focus on student voice and youth leadership made YCfD a truly meaningful experience not just for me or my peers in the group, but for all the students that our work touched as well.

Draw Conclusions (Findings). Once we felt that we had exhausted our data analysis, we grouped our themes together with their corresponding evidence and drew *findings*. Figure 5.3 displays an excerpt of findings from our year 2 study along with student responses as evidence to support the themes/findings.

Due to the overwhelming amount of data, time constraints, and the iterative nature of data analysis, it is improbable that we caught every theme or considered all pieces of the data. We acknowledge that there were outliers that we did not get a chance to negotiate and address. However, this was a powerful process for our youth. Not only did it develop key academic skills (reading, writing, high-level analysis, research), many students commented on feeling that the findings were affirming to student experiences. This was a transformative process that gave credibility to student voice, allowing them to articulate what they already knew that was grounded in research.

YCfD Found 8 Themes From the Data

1. Students in high-achieving schools felt an overwhelming pressure to succeed.
2. White students generally felt they were treated fairly.
3. Students who were at a school with a concentrated white population viewed disproportionality as individual failures of people of color.
4. Black, Latinx, and Muslim students felt isolated at predominantly white and Asian schools.
5. Students in predominantly Black and Latinx schools did not have a favorable schooling experience.
6. Students at "elite" schools felt the schooling system works perfectly fine.
7. The absence of teachers of color impacted the schooling experience for students and staff.
8. Students wanted "diversity."

Figure 5.3. Findings

Evidence to support theme 1:

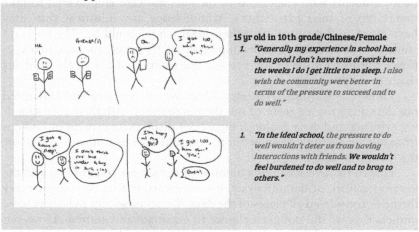

Evidence to support theme 2:

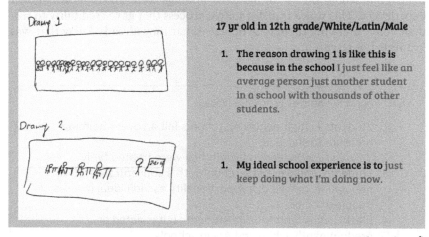

(continued)

Although we finished our project with powerful conclusions, this process was not easy. It took hours of work and additional sessions to complete. It took teamwork and adult-youth solidarity. We spent many Friday nights breaking down data and having tough conversations for hours. But we believe we are better because of it. The work we put in was the work we got out. Equity work takes time, effort, dedication, and commitment. This cannot be replaced by a one-day workshop or one

Figure 5.3. (continued)

Evidence to support theme 4:

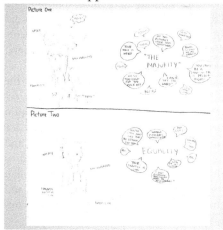

15/9/Black/Puerto Rican/Female

1. *"In this school, it's as if I'm isolated because of what I look like and who I identify as. They bring up annoying stereotypes that are nowhere near true! It's also like some people pity me and even try to show "sympathy" for no reason. It's also like they don't want me to be who I really am. Instead, they try to make up some "character" they want me to pretend I am. It's a toxic environment."*

2. *"The ideal school for me is a place where I'll be accepted. I'm not such a social person but still, I'll feel comfortable talking to an being around others. No one says those dumb "funny" stereotypes. Everyone is "good vibes" or just doesn't want to make anyone uncomfortable or like they don't belong. It's a fun, but smart environment."*

Evidence to support theme 5:

16/11/Caribbean/Male

1. I feel imprisoned in school I wish I didn't have to stand in line to be searched to get into school and then be held to a strict code as to what I have to do during the day I wish the teachers would help us in our individual learning styles than having to be forced to work in ways that don't work for me.

1. A fluid environment that promotes an environment that makes kids excited to be in and participate.

"courageous conversation." It is a lifelong commitment. And the work doesn't stop at the end of the project.

At the end of this process, youth participant Mia reflected:

YCfD was a space where we learned to name and identify the root causes and underlying systems that created the educational experiences we were having. It allowed for analyzing and dissecting the historical, systemic, local, and national conversations around the education system—specifically in disproportionality and segregation in race, socioeconomic status, and disability. These conversations then allowed for honesty and vulnerability in our own personal experiences. Beyond these impactful conversations, we also did YPAR at our own schools with an arts-based approach of asking students how they felt in their schools and not only asking about quantifiable data. Our quantitative data came from demographic and disciplinary records provided by our schools' administration. We also analyzed the same data for the city, state, and nation. Our findings and conclusions led to making policy recommendations and proposals as well as joining conversations with education leaders. Overall, the process of learning about the foundational context for personal experiences, researching the manifestations of systemic issues, and then presenting them in policy proposals or in key conversations helped us to begin to humanize data rather than allow the data to be one dimensional. This work was important because it allowed us to turnkey our findings and understandings back to our respective communities and also to broader conversations in the educational policy sphere.

CONCLUSION

Overall, we learned a great deal from this process. Through this project the students had the opportunity to *rewrite and re-right* their position in history (Smith, 1999). As participant researchers, the youth rightly "[told their] stories from the past, [reclaimed] the past, giving testimony to the injustices of the past [which] are all strategies commonly employed by indigenous peoples struggling for justice" (Smith 1999, p. 35). It is not enough to use students' emotions and trauma in order to produce work adults should have been doing from the beginning. Youth have been historically disenfranchised and decentered from their own education, and it is now time to partner with students to create a more humanizing education system.

Key Takeaways

From building community to establishing a solid partnership and then executing the YPAR project, it is our hope that this work will encourage educators to listen to youth and form genuine youth-adult partnerships where we can begin to address issues such as disproportionality in solidarity.

In this chapter, we discussed:

1. Forming a contact zone
2. Establishing a close community

3. Political education
4. Youth-led research and analysis of school disparities

We hope this inspires you to take advantage of the knowledge your students have of schooling and disproportionality. The process and tools outlined above worked for YCfD to engage youth to be a part of systems change work. We share this with you in hopes that this guide establishes and grows youth work in your own district. Again, this work is not a one-size-fits-all, but all the tools and procedures offered are best practices to building more culturally responsive, critically conscious learning environments. Youth have always been key leaders in pushing for change. As school leadership works to serve all students, it is necessary to amplify their voices. We believe that including young people in this work is a key component for enacting change to create more equitable and just schools for every child.

CRITICAL QUESTIONS

1. How can you strengthen youth-adult relationships?
2. How can you get youth more involved in addressing disproportionality in your schools?
3. Who else can you partner with to build support for a YPAR project?
4. How can youth be a part of presenting information and policy recommendations at a school or a district level?

Conclusion

Despite the resounding critiques of K–12 and higher education from political conservatives who regard public education as "too woke," we argue that the promise of formal education as the "great equalizer" has fallen short. Just shy of the 70th anniversary of *Brown v. Board of Education* Supreme Court decision to desegregate schools, Bettina Love (2023) wrote in *Education Week*:

> If you examine public school data on funding or who among our students are surveilled, policed, and suspended or have the opportunity to take AP classes, extracurriculars, and other forms of enrichment, our public education system was never woke; I am not sure if it was ever awake. Black students make up less than 15 percent of K–12 public school students—yet 30 percent of public school students who are suspended, expelled, and arrested. (2023)

Yet, we are in a moment where politicians are eliciting book bans on literature that showcases people of color as protagonists or LGBTQIA+ content, or that addresses issues of race and inequity (Friedman & Johnson, 2022), and remove critical scholarship from African American history courses (Hartocollis & Fawcett, 2023). Schools are still racially segregated across (Frankenberg et al., 2019) and within schools (Francis & Darity, 2021), and zero tolerance policies continue to perpetuate racial inequities (Shange, 2019) and feed the school-to-prison pipeline (Hemez et al., 2020). The Sentencing Project documented that

> Black youth are more than four times as likely to be detained or committed in juvenile facilities as their white peers [. . .]. Nationally, the youth placement rate was 114 per 100,000. The Black youth placement rate was 315 per 100,000, compared to the white youth placement rate of 72 per 100,000. (Rovner, 2021).

We were confronted by this grim reality during our YPAR study (see Chapter 5) when a 16-year-old Black male student drew a picture of himself behind bars of a jail cell that was captioned,

I feel imprisoned in school. I wish I didn't have to stand in line to be searched to get into school and then be held to a strict code as to what I have to be during the day. I wish the teachers would help us in our individual learning styles than having to be forced to work in ways that don't work for me.

The alternative of what he *wanted* schools to be was:

A fluid environment that promotes an environment that makes kids excited to be in and participate.

We have learned from our youth that, more than ever, restorative practices are necessary. Educators must look within themselves in order to make radical changes from the self to the systemic level. In the spirit of the legacy of education for liberation, it is necessary to create avenues for Black joy and Black genius to flourish (Muhammad, 2020) to reach educational justice for all children and their families in schools. Achieving this goal must include connecting self to system.

FROM SELF TO SYSTEM

In the wake of the murder of George Floyd in 2020, which was followed by a supposed national racial reckoning, it has never been clearer that moving toward equity and justice in schools must leverage both the individual and the system. The work of moving from *self to system* is about connecting beliefs, policies, procedures, and practices that are present in schools to first dismantle the disproportionality that exists while at the same time forging a new path forward—one that is race-conscious and culturally conscious and that positions students at the center. We deeply believe in educators' need to develop consistent and more deliberate critical self-reflection. We also believe that at the same time, historically racist policies and school-based structures have to be dismantled (Hernández et al., 2023). *Both* are not only possible, but imperative.

At the end of Chapter 1, we offered the ingredients needed to *set the table* for systemic racial equity shifts. We highlighted the steps to cultivate adult learning spaces that:

1) are bound by community norms that hold individuals accountable to the collective's growth;
2) work to continuously name the *elephants in the room*, centering those most impacted in effort to disrupt the status quo and white normative school spaces; and

3) don't retreat when met by a *racial equity tension*, but instead use
   this language and understanding to propel the work forward.

Once the table is set (and continually tended to, adapted, and rein-
forced), building institutional critical reflection becomes necessary to the
foundation of a culturally responsive school and district environment
(Khalifa, 2018). In Chapter 2 we walked through key understandings of
culturally responsive education and then tangible practices to be employed
by educators to actively do the work of building equity-based critical reflection. Our goal is that these processes kickstart a continued inquiry and
grappling that ultimately better serve our students' schooling experience. So
often when we engage districts in equity work, we hear the refrain, "I never
thought about this before!," which only heightens the necessity for tangible
processes that serve to move an equity mindset from a choice most often
missed to an imperative and starting point for any school-based decision.

Moreover, as we look at several decades of education reform, we
can see that leapfrogging the self-excavation journey most often leads
to flimsy policies or surface-level efforts at building student-to-teacher
relationships. To that end, we intentionally positioned the root cause processes identified in Chapter 3 and 4 after the CR-SE awareness and understanding building outlined in Chapters 1 and 2. Without doing the
self-excavation work, individuals center problematic beliefs that stall equity progress. This also reinforces policies and practices that disproportionately impact the same children and families. This pushback can look
like educators refuting the disproportionality data, not acknowledging the
role of racism and anti-Blackness, or wanting to focus on "all students"
when Black students are experiencing disproportionate harm and continue
to not have an equitable education.

Yes, we want every district to move through the root cause analysis
tools and deeply investigate their disaggregated data, while also starting
with the voices of historically and currently marginalized young folks and
families. That said, data analysis without an understanding of the impact
of self and systems has the potential to further harm the individuals and
communities we are purporting to support. District leaders and educators supporting equity efforts need to be clear about the necessary work
to create readiness for a root cause analysis—readiness that will not only
bring inequities to light but that will move forward with actual systemic
change. Tangible, systemic change is about strategic moves like the creation of a multiyear district equity plan that outlines sustainable practices
centering children and families who are most impacted. Moreover, to
shift systems, the plan is built with internal and external accountability
measures, ensuring that there is an active and ongoing process moving the
district toward more equitable practices.

Our Black youth and young folks with other marginalized identities have always been in the position of both having to advocate for their own inclusion while continuing to be harmed by a system built to exclude them. If we are bringing young people to the table to provide their voice and experience, we have to believe them. Too many of the adults in our system fail to do this and continue to blame children for the harm that is committed by adults. We offer Chapter 5 as a guide to shift our approach to students as leaders—to recognize the accountability we have as adult educators to reconfigure our classroom and school spaces to be student-led and critically conscious. One of the key tenets connected to Gloria Ladson-Billing's (1995) original framings of culturally responsive pedagogy is *teacher as facilitator*. When adults have an embedded practice of culturally responsive self-reflection, they recognize that the most powerful moments in the classroom come when they step back and let students lead.

COMMITMENT TO DOING THE WORK: VOICES FROM CSC CR-SE WORK

We have supported and witnessed various educators and districts who have made a commitment to stay on track in doing the work (see Hernández et al., 2023). They have understood that addressing their disproportionality is not a quick fix and have leaned into an ongoing long-term commitment. In this next section, we present reflections from educators over the years who have participated in our trainings. The majority of districts we have partnered with consist of predominantly white educators. Through interviews, participants have spoken about the personal and professional transformation CR-SE trainings have had in their lives. All the educators interviewed are white cisgender females or males. They highlighted that CR-SE trainings offered:

1) a developed process to engage in continual self-reflection about social identity, power, and privilege;
2) a practice of critical self-reflection to continually evaluate their practices; and
3) a pathway to further training opportunities in their school and district.

Continual Self-Reflection About Social Identity, Power, and Privilege

Educators shared that the CR-SE training offers the conditions to engage in a process of continual self-reflection on their social identity, power, and privilege. Participants connected their identities, power, and privilege to their practices. The self-work to reflect on and engage CR-SE practices (see Chapters 1 and 2) warrants that educators work through self-excavation, including grappling with their lack of acknowledgment, understanding, and denial of their race and racism. Kate, an elementary school teacher, wrestles with their privilege of racelessness and reconciles that their students' are impacted by race daily. In their reflection, Kate stresses the agency they have as an educator to shift their classroom culture:

> I remember it was one of the CR-SE meetings . . . last summer, thinking about "when did you notice your race?" And I was really embarrassed because I think it was in college and that moment was important for me because I realized that a lot of my students are aware of their race every single day . . . it's important to realize that other students . . . other adults even, other than yourself, have to think about their race every single day. Being aware of that, being able to change the way you conduct yourself and being able to change your classroom culture, because you know that burden is on so many other students has been really important for me.

Similarly, Sarah, an elementary school teacher, demonstrates how the work of self-reflection can lead to a greater understanding of biased-based beliefs and practices that are harmful to students of color, and how this work has the power to shift beliefs and practices:

> Racism wasn't me. It was other white people. Yeah, but like, not me. But then I think through my work and CR-SE [work], I kind of realized you know, having a white father who defended Black men and having a white mother who taught mainly Black students. I think that a lot of that white saviorism was in me and thinking that my job as a white person was to help Black people, or help Black students or help these people. And I think that that can really get kind of misconstrued into thinking that it's my job as a white person to do this and kind of getting into all that was something I really had to dig through.

Critical Self-Reflection to Evaluate Practice

Educators stated that the CR-SE training gave them the foundation to consistently look for and create opportunities to engage in critical self-reflection practices, including changing instructional materials, instructional practices, and implementing practices of self-accountability. Additionally, this process encouraged educators to challenge white, normative structures of schooling. Further, this led to educators engaging in additional CR-SE training in their districts and schools, or being directly involved in developing trainings.

Cindy, another elementary school teacher, shares how their critical self-reflection drives the daily decisions they make about lessons and their connection to students' experiences and outcomes:

> I think that [what] really sticks with me is that critical thinking and really questioning like, why am I doing this? . . . it just makes me think about each lesson and think about, well, what is the purpose of this lesson? How am I pushing my students' critical thinking, how am I responding to where they're coming from? And is this lesson based on my culture? Is it based on what I expect to see? Or is it based on what I know about my kids?

Creating Further Training Opportunities

Engaging in this process is motivating for educators to consistently look for and create opportunities to engage themselves and others to continue their training or support district training efforts. Such efforts hold the potential to further build district and school capacity and sustain practices.

Amy, an elementary school teacher, speaks to their motivation to further engage trainings to expand their classroom practices:

> I am going to continue to do the CR-SE technical training . . . Once you do [the training] you realize how much more you have to keep doing . . . What more can I dig deeper with and what does that look like in my classroom?

Allison highlights their role developing in district professional learnings in an effort to build internal capacity:

> Right now we're developing professional development for our specific district so we're taking what we did in the CR-SE program and saying "Okay, you could spend a whole day on the racial identity model, you could spend a whole day on microaggressions you could—taking things that we did in an hour and saying how do we turn this into a 5-hour day? I'm working on developing those smaller branches of professional development where you can dig deeper into one particular aspect.

As highlighted in the quotes above, efforts to build individual educator capacity have created the readiness to build district- and school-wide systems to implement CR-SE practices.

Building Capacity: Train the Trainer Model

Our Train the Trainer (TTT) model (Hernández et al., 2023) builds internal capacity for educators to develop skills to lead CR-SE in their respective districts and schools, which includes further professional learning, coaching, and creating school-based equity teams. For systemic shifts to occur, individuals must be trained first, followed by building the capacity of educators to lead the work. Educators who have engaged in the co-facilitation model speak to the ways the TTT model impacted them and their district/school. Specifically, co-facilitators explained how they developed a collaborative culture within the co-facilitation team and beyond, alongside the skills needed to lead the CR-SE work in their respective schools and districts.

Ted, an administrator, highlights the TTT model's effectiveness in preparing teams to implement CR-SE and model a structure for co-facilitator feedback:

> I don't know if we would have had the success that we feel that this team has had if we didn't participate in the model, the way that it was set up. And what I mean by that is scheduling those pre-meetings right prior to this reviewing the concept, we're doing [each] point so that we're able to prepare going into those meetings or those sessions with what we wanted to cover. Similarly, the debrief sessions were just as important too. I think the three of us [referring to co-facilitators] were very open and honest with each other, to not only be able to provide feedback to each other, honest and open feedback, but then to receive it as well. I think the [associate] does a great job facilitating those conversations. Also, we each set goals for ourselves. And I know it was helpful for me to reflect on "okay, what was that?" "That goal that we had in the previous session?" So that I could specifically focus on that goal going into the next session. So I think just the intentionality. Let's review and provide feedback, honest feedback. That our feelings aren't going to be hurt, or anything like that. We were comfortable kind of calling each other out.

Kristina, another administrator, tells how the TTT model created collaboration among the co-facilitation team and opportunities to support educators engaging in the work after sessions:

> In the work every month that we've done with [the CR-SE] lead learner, each of us takes a very active role, either co-facilitating some of the content or leading it on our own, and then we take turns supporting within the training. But then, outside of the [CR-SE training], all of the facilitators have had the opportunity to kind of serve as another sense of support. So quite often teachers who participated in the CR-SE training will want to follow up with one of us to kind of process something, or something else is happening within the school community and they want to process it. So they have leaned on us to help open up those conversations, help them identify tensions that they have in the room,

identify examples of harm, and begin conversations about what we can do to help repair, or at least acknowledge, that something has happened, and that we need to do something in terms of working together as a community.

The TTT model over time continues to build leaders who have the capacity to lead CR-SE trainings, create and implement truncated trainings, and practice and push their colleagues to center CR-SE and equity in their work.

DISTRICT EXAMPLE BUILDING EDUCATOR AND SYSTEMIC CAPACITY

Several of our partnering districts have engaged in building structures to shift mindsets, policies, and procedures to develop and sustain CR-SE practices. This has included building leadership capacity through the TTT model, building district- and school-level equity teams, developing inquiry-based CR-SE practices, embedding CR-SE practices in their classrooms and departmental meetings, and using book studies to continue to support educators who have already been trained. One example of a district that continues to such an approach is Port Central.

Port Central School District has been engaged in the TTT model for 3 years. The co-facilitators on this team have been white cisgender males. Two of the males have been part of the TTT for 3 years, and one for 1 year. The co-facilitators highlighted the impact of the TTT model on their personal and professional lives, and how it has translated into an impact on their district.

Elmer, who is a school counselor, underscores how the personal transformation of the training and their co-facilitator role has transferred to their professional growth:

> I don't think I'm exaggerating when I say that this training and being a facilitator changed my life in the course of my professional career. I think in the way that we learn the material, and then we're kind of empowered to take risks and try it, and push ourselves and get uncomfortable. I think that model really helped us grow an enormous amount and be the best educators in this way that we could.

Josh, an administrator, speaks to how the district is approaching systematizing CR-SE. The district has enough capacity to implement the model locally through educators who have been trained and those who have engaged in the TTT model. Further, their focus is on further developing school building–based teams:

I think back to the structure that had been set up and how it's really a coaching and a supportive model, which I think we found a lot of success with. I think, obviously, our goal is always going to build capacity. Our district is shifting next year to offering the [CR-SE] training sessions in district. And so far we won't be participating in the co-facilitator model for next year. . . . We've also identified some people within the district to lead this work so that we can get the word more in the buildings. And we're looking at that as a way to bolster into supporting those building-based teams.

As mentioned in the last quote, by building internal capacity through the co-facilitation model, the district will start to independently implement our CR-SE trainings. Port has also developed truncated CR-SE trainings that are implemented during the superintendent's conference day. Additionally, they have developed a district-wide team and school-level CR-SE committees. The following educators, who have only participated in the training, speak to the ways that the district is moving from training individuals to implementing the work. The importance of getting to a place to successfully implement CR-SE work in districts warrants building both individual and TTT capacity, messaging a district's commitment to the work, and developing structures (e.g., building-level implementation teams).

John, a white elementary school teacher, discusses how much they have seen shifts in the district and school in CR-SE. It hasn't been about just building a critical mass of educators trained in CR-SE; it has also included staff engaging differently with the work.

I think for me, with each passing year we get here in the building, that we get closer to that critical mass. That it becomes much more unacceptable to not be on board than it is. In conversations that we hear you can hear people thinking about equity and CR-SE in ways that I certainly didn't hear at the beginning of this work. I think we've become much better at being honest and avoiding those like detours and falling back into places of comfort. I think there's a much higher willingness of the staff to challenge themselves.

Elmer, who is a co-facilitator, shares the critical shifts they have seen as a school counselor, including prioritizing CR-SE by communicating the importance of CR-SE, creating structures, and building CR-SE into daily practices:

At every level of administration it's been made very explicit that this is a priority, and it's something that the district values. There's been nothing that has been left up to doubt. And I also think some structural things that the district has done with the elementary schedule of putting in a social-emotional learning block every day, that has really given us the capability to use a CR-SE focus. We are in our daily community circles. We're having conversations about race. We're using those community circles to have honest conversations when incidents happen, so I think, the district has made a clear verbal commitment. But, they've backed it up with structural changes to our schedule, too.

Port's effort in building critical mass has also focused on starting to build CR-SE work into school buildings. Part of this process has entailed creating CR-SE committees. One of the school committees centers on developing CR-SE lessons. Janine, another elementary school teacher, shares how the CR-SE committee is being implemented in their school:

My school has a CR-SE committee that a couple of teachers have signed up to be on . . . Every month or two we create a lesson to share with the staff . . . the expectation [is] that teachers are going to use it in their classrooms. So when the month came for me to plan one, I said, "Okay, I think I want to do like *Black joy*," celebrating Black culture. And I planned the lesson with the [CR-SE] work that we had done together in mind, and one of the teachers that is also on the committee taught a lesson, and she said it was the best it was through the CR-SE framework. . . . For the most part I read the book *Black Is a Rainbow Color* . . . The questions were like, "What kind of things do you see in your culture that are familiar to you? What is unfamiliar to you? How does it make you feel to see things that are familiar? How does it make you feel to see things that are unfamiliar?"

CONCLUSION AND WHAT IS NEXT?

After reading this book and to move forward with your work and the intersecting equity efforts in your district, we hope you continue to grapple with the following questions to move both self and system:

Self:

• What does critical self-reflection look like for me?
• How am I processing the impact my social identities have on my students?
• What is my active reflective work that happens before and after the school day?
• How do I navigate the ways my own power and privilege impact students and the school environment?

- In what ways do I de-center my own perspective and values to further center students?
- Have I developed a practice of checking in with students (particularly students holding identities that are being pushed to the margins) to actively listen, believe, and respond to how they are feeling in school?
- Have I developed a practice of checking in with families (particularly students holding identities that are being pushed to the margins) to actively listen, believe, and respond to how they are feeling about their child's school/classroom experience?

System:

- How does my personal work connect to the needed systemic work?
- Am I actively working toward changing a system that continues to fail Black, Indigenous/Native, and other young folks of color? How so?
- What policies are shifting based on the work my team and I are a part of?
- As a school/district system, are our educators all aware of the disproportionality that exists and continuously monitoring for improvement?
- Has a long-term equity plan been established and does everyone know our role in making systemic change?

The work of *self to system* requires educators to start with self. Without engaging in self-work, practices fall short to respond to students of color (in particular, Black, Latinx, and Indigenous/Native), students with an IEP, and multilingual learners and students holding these intersecting identities. To that end, the push remains to engage educators in a community of practice, engaging in difficult conversations that are race-conscious in their approach. Further, the ongoing work of dismantling disproportionality demands that educators be brave and bold, and practice ongoing individual and institutional critical self-reflection. We can no longer act out of fear and complicity given that our children's lives are on the line every day, but instead we must *go for broke* and put forth the work needed to create more loving and trusting school environments.

Glossary

Indicator 4A	Known as a significant discrepancy in the *rate* of suspensions and expulsions of students with disabilities for greater than 10 days in a school year.
Indicator 4B	Known as a significant discrepancy in the *rates* of out-of-school suspensions and expulsions of greater than 10 days in a school year of students with disabilities by **race and ethnicity.**
Microaggressions	Commonplace verbal or behavioral indignities, whether intentional or unintentional, which communicate hostile, derogatory, or negative racial slights and insults (Sue et al., 2007).
Significant Disproportionality	Highlighted by race/ethnicity in the incidence, duration, and type of disciplinary actions, including suspensions and expulsions set through a relative risk ratio.
Social identity	Social identity refers to individuals' self-categorization in relation to their group membership. These categorizations can be assigned, or individuals can be born into them. Individuals claim identity groups based on their physical, social, and mental characteristics. They are sometimes obvious and clear, sometimes not obvious and unclear, often self-claimed, and frequently ascribed by others.

Endnotes

Chapter 2

1. In a capitalist society, ownership of property affords certain rights and privileges, including the creation of generational wealth.

2. Harris argues that those who possess whiteness maintain privileges in ways similar to those who own property. Whiteness as property highlights the systemic ways that white people have advantages, including access to better education, political power, and employment opportunities.

3. The white gaze highlights the dominant position and power dynamics where whiteness is considered the norm or the standard against which all other perspectives are judged.

4. From Gloria Ladson-Billings's 1995 *But That's Just Good Teaching! The Case for Culturally Relevant Pedagogy.*

Chapter 3

1. S.M.A.R.T goals refer to goals that are specific, measurable, achievable, relevant, and time-bound. Defining these parameters connected to a goal helps ensure that objectives are attainable within a certain time frame.

Chapter 4

1. Fountas and Pinnell is a cohesive multi-text approach to literacy instruction for students K–6 that includes benchmark assessment to determines students' reading levels. Their material can be found here: https://www.fountasandpinnell.com/

2. The Dignity for All Students Act (DASA) is a policy in New York State seeking to provide the state's public elementary and secondary school students with a safe and supportive environment free from discrimination, intimidation, taunting, harassment, and bullying on school property, a school bus, and/or at a school function. https://www.nysed.gov/student-support-services/dignity-all -students-act-dasa

3. Second Step is a classroom-based social emotional learning program.

Chapter 5

1. Positionality is the social and political context that creates your identity in terms of race, class, gender, sexuality, and ability status. Positionality also describes how your identity influences, and potentially biases, your understanding of and outlook on the world.

2. Whereas ally-ship is performative or self-glorifying, co-conspirators use their power and privilege to stand in solidarity with vulnerable groups to confront anti-Blackness and injustice. A co-conspirator functions as a verb, not a noun (Love, 2019, p. 117).

3. There are five boroughs in New York City (Bronx, Brooklyn, Manhattan, Queens, and Staten Island).

Chapter 6

1. The Center for School Change (CSC) is a center that became a natural extension of the CfD post–closing out CfD.

References

Alim, H. S., Paris, D., & Wong, C. P. (2020). Culturally sustaining pedagogy: A critical framework for centering communities. In N. S. Nasir, C. D. Lee, R. Pea, & M. McKinney de Royston (Eds.,) *Handbook of the cultural foundations of learning* (pp. 261–276). Routledge.

Baldwin, J. (1963). A talk to teachers. In R. Simonson & S. Walker (Eds.), *Multiculturalism literacy* (pp. 3–12). Graywolf Press.

Bell, D. A. (2008). *Race, racism & American law* (6th ed.). Aspen Publishers.

Bell, J., Zaino, K., & Sealey-Ruiz, Y. (2022). Diggin' in the racial literacy crates. *Equity & Excellence in Education*, 56(1), 1–14. https://doi.org/10.1080/10 665684.2022.2064354

Bonilla-Silva, E. (2017). *Racism without racists: Color-blind racism and the persistence of racial inequality in America* (4th ed). Rowman & Littlefield Publishers.

Bryk, A. S., Bender Sebring, P., Allensworth, E., Luppescu, S., & Easton, J. Q. (2010). *Organizing for school improvement: Lessons from Chicago*. University of Chicago Press.

Bryk, A., Gomez, L. M., Grunow, A., & LeMahieu, P. (2015). *Learning to improve: How America's schools can get better at getting better*. Harvard Education Press.

Cammarota, J., & Fine, M. (Eds.). (2008). *Revolutionizing education: Youth participatory action research in motion*. Routledge.

Carter, P. L., Skiba, R., Arrendondo, M., I., & Pollock, M. (2017). You can't fix what you don't look at: Acknowledging race in addressing racial disparities. *Urban Education, 52*(2), 207–235.

DiAngelo, R. (2018). *White fragility: Why it's so hard for white people to talk about racism*. Beacon Press.

Fergus, E. (2017). *Solving disproportionality and achieving equity: A leader's guide to using data to change hearts and minds*. Sage Publications.

Fergus, E., & Ahram, R. (2009). *Racial/ethnic disproportionality in special education: Data analysis workbook*. NYU Steinhardt Metropolitan Center for Urban Education. https://greatlakesequity.org/resource/data-analysis-work book-racialethnic-disproportionality-special-education

Francis, D. V., & Darity, W. A. (2021). Separate and unequal under one roof: How the legacy of racialized tracking perpetuates within-school segregation. *RSF: The Russell Sage Foundation Journal of the Social Sciences*, 7(1), 187–202. https://doi.org/10.7758/rsf.2021.7.1.11

Frankenberg, E., Ee, J., Ayscue, J. B., & Orfield, G. (2019). *Harming our common future*. Center for Education and Civil Rights. https://www.civilrights project.ucla.edu/research/k-12-education/integration-and-diversity/harming -our-common-future-americas-segregated-schools-65-years-after-brown/ Brown-65-050919v4-final.pdf

Freire, P., & Macedo, D. (1970). *Pedagogy of the oppressed, 30th anniversary edition* (M. B. Ramos, Trans). Continuum.

Friedman, J., & Farid Johnson, N. (2022). *Banned in the USA: The growing movement to ban books*. PEN America. https://pen.org/report/banned-usa-growing -movement-to-censor-books-in-schools/

Fullan, M., & Quinn, J. (2016). *Coherence: The right drivers in action for schools, districts, and systems*. Sage Publications.

Ginwright, S. (2015). *Hope and healing in urban education*. Routledge.

Glaser, B. G., & Strauss, A. L. (1968). *The discovery of grounded theory: Strategies for qualitative research*. Aldine.

Gorski, P. (2019). Avoiding racial equity detours. *Educational Leadership, 76*(7), 56–61.

Gorski, P., DuBose, M., & Swalwell, K. (2022). Trading baby steps for equity leaps. *Educational Leadership, 79*(5), 26–31. https://www.ascd.org/el/articles /trading-baby-steps-for-big-equity-leaps

Hall, E. T. (1976). *Beyond culture*. Anchor Press/Doubleday.

Hammond, Z. L. (2015). *Culturally responsive teaching & the brain*. Corwin Press.

Harris, C. I. (1993). Whiteness as property. *Harvard Law Review, 106*(8), 1707–1791. https://doi.org/10.2307/1341787

Hart, R. (1992). Children's participation: From tokenism to citizenship. International Child Development Centre. https://www.unicef-irc.org/publications /100-childrens-participation-from-tokenism-to-citizenship.html

Hartocollis, A., & Fawcett, E. (2023, February 1). The College Board strips down its A.P. curriculum for African American Studies. *The New York Times*. https://www.nytimes.com/2023/02/01/us/college-board-advanced-place ment-african-american-studies.html

Hemez, P., Brent, J. J., & Mowen, T. J. (2020). Exploring the school-to-prison pipeline: How school suspensions influence incarceration during young adulthood. *Youth Violence and Juvenile Justice, 18*(3), 235–255. https://doi.org /10.1177/1541204019880945

Hernández, M. G., Lopez, D., & Swier, R. (2023). *Dismantling disproportionality: A culturally responsive and sustaining systems approach*. Teachers College Press.

Jackson, K. R., Fixsen, D., & Ward, C. (2018). *Four domains for rapid school improvement: An implementation framework*. National Implementation Research Network. https://files.eric.ed.gov/fulltext/ED606092.pdf

Khalifa, M. (2018). *Culturally responsive school leadership*. Harvard Education Press.

Klingner, J. K., Artiles, A. J., Kozleski, E., Harry, B., Zion, S., Tate, W., Zamora Duncán, G., & Riley, D. (2005). Addressing the disproportionate representation of culturally and linguistically diverse students in special education through culturally responsive educational systems. *Education Policy Analysis Archives, 13*(38), 2–40.

Kozleski, E. B., & Artiles, A. J. (2012). Technical assistance as inquiry: Using activity theory methods to engage equity in educational practice communities. In G. Canella & S. Steinberg (Eds.), *Critical Qualitative Research reader* (pp. 408–419). Peter Lang.

Ladson-Billings, G. (1995). But that's just good teaching! The case for culturally relevant pedagogy. *Theory Into Practice, 34*(3), 159–165. http://www.jstor.org/stable/1476635

Ladson-Billings, G. (1998). Just what is critical race theory and what's it doing in a nice field like education? *International Journal of Qualitative Studies in Education, 11*(1), 7–24. https://doi.org/10.1080/095183998236863

Ladson-Billings, G.. (2021). *Culturally relevant pedagogy: Asking a different question*. Teachers College Press.

Ladson-Billings, G., & Tate, W. F. (1995). Toward a critical race theory of education. *Teachers College Record, 97*(1), 47–68. https://doi.org/10.1177/016146819509700104

LeFrançois, B. A. (2014). Adultism. In T. Teo (Ed.), *Encyclopedia of Critical Psychology* (pp. 47–49). Springer. https://doi.org/10.1007/978-1-4614-5583-7_6

Love, B. (2019). *We want to do more than survive: Abolitionist teaching and the pursuit of educational freedom*. Beacon Press.

Love, B. L. (2023, July 14). No, public education isn't too woke. It's barely even awake. *Education Week*. https://www.edweek.org/leadership/opinion-no-public-education-isnt-too-woke-its-barely-even-awake/2023/07

Love, B., & Sealey-Ruiz, Y. (2019, April 20). *Bettina Love more than ally* [Video]. Schomburg Center for Research in Black Culture. C-SPAN. https://www.c-span.org/video/?c4964262/user-clip-bettina-love-ally

Lucas, S. R., & Berends, M. (2002). Sociodemographic diversity, correlated achievement, and de facto tracking. *Sociology of Education, 75*(4), 328–348. https://doi.org/10.2307/3090282

Lykes, M. B., & Mallona, A. (2008). Towards transformational liberation: Participatory and action research praxis. In P. Reason & H. Bradbury (Eds.), *The SAGE Handbook of Action Research* (2nd ed., pp. 260–292). Sage Publications. https://www.researchgate.net/publication/260434575_Towards_Transformational_Liberation_Participatory_and_Action_Research_Praxis

Malone, H., McAlister, S., & Perez, W. Y. (2023). Navigating intersectionality and positionality within Black and Latinx youth organizing spaces. *Youth & Society, 0,(0)*, 1–20. https://doi.org/10.1177/0044118X231159710

McCarty, T., & Lee, T. (2014). Critical culturally sustaining/revitalizing pedagogy and Indigenous education sovereignty. *Harvard Educational Review, 84*(1), 101–124. https://doi.org/10.17763/haer.84.1.q83746nl5pj34216

McIntosh, K., & Goodman, S. (2016). *Integrated multi-tiered systems of support: Blending RtI and PBIS*. Guildford Press.

Milner, R., Liu, K., & Ball, A. F. (2020). Critical counter-narratives as transformative methodology for educational equity. *Review of Research in Education, 44*, 269–300.

Mitra, D. L. (2009). Collaborating with students: Building youth-adult partnerships in schools. *American Journal of Education, 115*(3), 407–436. https://doi.org/10.1086/597488

Morris, M. W. (2016). *Pushout: The criminalization of Black girls in schools.* The New Press.

Muhammad, G. (2020). *Cultivating genius: An equity framework for culturally and historically responsive literacy.* Scholastic Teaching Resources.

NAACP Legal Defense Fund. (2023). *What is Critical Race Theory: FAQs and more explained.* Legal Defense Fund. https://www.naacpldf.org/critical-race-theory-faq/

Odom Pough, N. (2021). A flaw in the foundation. *Learning for Justice,* Spring (66), 24–27. https://www.learningforjustice.org/magazine/spring-2021/a-flaw-in-the-foundation

Oto, R. (2023). "This is for us, not them": Troubling adultism through a pedagogy of solidarity in youth organizing and activism. *Theory & Research in Social Education,* 1–29. https://doi.org/10.1080/00933104.2023.2208538

Paris, D. (2012). Culturally sustaining pedagogy: A needed change in stance, terminology, and practice. *Educational Researcher, 41*(3), 93–97. https://doi.org/10.3102/0013189X12441244

Paris, D. (2019). Naming beyond the white settler colonial gaze in educational research. *International Journal of Qualitative Studies in Education, 32*(3), 217–224.

Paris, D. (2021). Culturally sustaining pedagogies and our futures. *The Educational Forum, 85*(4), 364–376. https://doi.org/10.1080/00131725.2021.1957634

Paris, D., & Alim, H. S. (Eds.). (2017). *Culturally sustaining pedagogies: Teaching and learning for justice in a changing world.* Teachers College Press.

Picower, B. (2009). The unexamined whiteness of teaching: How white teachers maintain and enact dominant racial ideologies. *Race Ethnicity and Education, 12*(2), 197–215.

Pollock, M. (2004). *Colormute: Race talk dilemmas in an American high school.* Princeton University Press.

Pollock, M., Deckman, S., Mira, M., & Shalaby, C. (2010). "But what can I do?": Three necessary tensions in teaching teachers about race. *Journal of Teacher Education, 61*(3), 211–224.

Renick, J., Abad, M. N., Van Es., E. A., & Mendoza, E. (2021). "It's all connected": Critical bifocality and the liminal practice of youth work. *Child & Youth Services, 42*(4), 349–373. https://doi.org/10.1080/0145935X.2021.1901571

Rovner, J. (2021). *Racial disparities in youth incarceration persist.* The Sentencing Project. https://www.sentencingproject.org/fact-sheet/racial-disparities-in-youth-incarceration-persist/

Rushovich, B. R., Bartley, L. H., Steward, R. K., & Bright, C. L. (2015). Technical assistance: A comparison between providers and recipients. *Human Service Organizations: Management, Leadership & Governance 39*(4), 362–379.

San Pedro, T., & Kinloch, V. (2017). Toward projects in humanization: Research on co-creating and sustaining dialogic relationships. *American Educational Research Journal, 54*(1), 373–394.

Sealey-Ruiz, Y. (2019). *Archaeology of self.* https://www.yolandasealeyruiz.com/archaeology-of-self

Shange, S. (2019). Black girl ordinary: Flesh, carcerality, and the refusal of ethnography. *Transforming Anthropology, 27*(1), 3–21. https://doi.org/10.1111/traa.12143

Smith, L. T. (1999). *Decolonizing methodologies: Research and Indigenous peoples* (2nd ed.). Zed Books.

Spencer, J. A., & Ullucci, K. (2023). *Anti-Blackness at school: Creating affirming educational spaces for African American students.* Teachers College Press.

Sue, D. W., Capodilupo, C. M., Torino, G. C., Bucceri, J. M., `Holder, A.M.B., Nadal, K. L., & Esquilin, M. (2007). Microaggressions in everyday life: Implications for clinical practice. *American Psychologist, 62* (4), 271–286.

Torre, M. E. (2008). Participatory action research in the contact zone. In J. Cammarota, & M. Fine, (Eds.), *Revolutionizing Education 5* (p. 363). Routledge.

UCLA School of Law Critical Race Studies Program. (2023). CRT Forward Tracking Project. https://crtforward.law.ucla.edu

U.S. Government Accountability Office. (2018). *K–12 education: Discipline disparities for Black students, boys, and students with disabilities.* https://www.gao.gov/products/GAO-18-258

Valdez, A., Takahashi, S., Krausen, K., Bowman, A., & Gurrola, E. (2020). *Getting better at getting more equitable: Opportunities and barriers for using continuous improvement to advance educational equity.* WestEd.

Valencia, R. R. (1997). *The evolution of deficit thinking: Educational thought and practice.* Falmer Press.

Index

Note: Page numbers followed by "n" indicate material in endnotes.

About the Authors

María G. Hernández has over a decade of experience providing technical assistance, training, and consultancy to districts, schools, and educational institutions to address race, ethnicity, language, and ability disproportionate outcomes. She coaches K–12 educators in developing systems that address disproportionality and equity by providing technical assistance and training. She supports districts and schools in building their capacity in culturally responsive sustaining education (CR-SE); creating equity visions, data-driven culture, instructional leadership, and positive school climate, family, and community engagement; and devising action plans with multiple districts in making changes to system policies and practices to develop equitable educational systems. Her approach of relying on evidence-based research, implementation science, and culturally responsive equitable systems and developing ongoing transformative relationships in educational institutions has led to shifting mindsets, policies, practices, and procedures. She holds an MSW and PhD in social welfare from the University of Wisconsin-Madison, and an MA in educational leadership from New York University.

Reed Swier is the co-director of Innovations in Equity and Systemic Change at The Metropolitan Center for Research on Equity and the Transformation of Schools at NYU Steinhardt, focused on promoting equity and opportunity in education. Currently, his work focuses on building capacity for educational institutions in understanding and responding to systems of inequality that disproportionately impact historically marginalized students and families. Reed has taught for over a decade in elementary schools in Oakland, California, and New York City. As a school administrator, Reed supported staff, students, and families by promoting culturally responsive teaching and developing a school culture philosophy and practice embedded in restorative approaches. In 2018, Reed lived in Scotland as a Fulbright Scholar, participating in the Fulbright Distinguished Awards in Teaching program, where he worked with local educators and University of Edinburgh students and faculty. Reed holds a BA from the University of Michigan, an MS in teaching grades 1–6 from

Pace University, and an MEd in learning and teaching from the Harvard
Graduate School of Education.

Hui-Ling S. Malone is an assistant professor of education at the University
of California Santa Barbara. Her research concerns culturally sustaining
pedagogies, critical pedagogy, youth activism, and youth participatory
action research in aims to advance equity in schools and their surrounding communities. She is a former secondary teacher who has taught in
Detroit, Michigan, and Los Angeles, California. She continued her work
in educational equity as a research assistant in The Metropolitan Center
for Research on Equity and the Transformation of Schools at NYU
Steinhardt, where she explored educational disparities throughout NYC
through a YPAR. Currently, Malone is a teacher educator and researcher
seeking to strengthen relationships among students, schools, and surrounding community members toward self-determination and social justice. She received her doctoral degree at New York University in teaching
and learning, with a focus on urban education.